THE PERSONAL EFFICIENCY PROGRAM

THE PERSONAL EFFICIENCY PROGRAM

How to Get Organized to Do More Work in Less Time

KERRY GLEESON

JOHN WILEY & SONS, INC.
New York • Chichester • Brisbane • Toronto • Singapore

Copyright © 1994 by Kerry Gleeson
Published by John Wiley & Sons, Inc.

All rights reserved. Published simultaneously in Canada.

Reproduction or translation of any part of this work beyond
that permitted by Section 107 or 108 of the 1976 United
States Copyright Act without the permission of the copyright
owner is unlawful. Requests for permission or further
information should be addressed to the Permissions Department,
John Wiley & Sons, Inc.

This publication is designed to provide accurate and authoritative
information in regard to the subject matter covered. It is sold
with the understanding that the publisher is not engaged in
rendering legal, accounting, or other professional services. If
legal advice or other expert assistance is required, the services
of a competent professional person should be sought.

Library of Congress Cataloging-in-Publication Data:

Gleeson, Kerry, 1948–
    The personal efficiency program : how to get organized to do more
work in less time / Kerry Gleeson.
        p.   cm.
    Includes index.
    ISBN 0-471-02058-3 (acid-free paper).—ISBN 0-471-02061-3 (pbk.
    : acid-free paper)—ISBN 0-471-19326-7 (mass market)
    1. Time management.   I. Title.
HD69.T54G58   1994
650.1—dc20   94-11922

Printed in the United States of America
10 9 8 7 6 5 4 3 2 1

In memory of my mother and father

PREFACE

I have worked with hundreds of successful and competent people over the years—executives from Sweden, managers from England, administrators from France, sales managers from the United States, and exporters from the Netherlands.

These people know how to get things done. They know what to do (doing the right thing or being effective) and how to best do it (doing things right or being efficient).

The focus of my work has been on the *process* of personal productivity. This book is a cumulation of my work with these very successful people who in some cases have taught me as much as I have taught them.

How important is it to know the principles of good work practices and better yet, to apply these principles? Charles Dickens once said:

I never could have done what I have done without the habits of punctuality, order and diligence, without the determination to concentrate myself on one subject at a time.

Dickens, being a writer, no doubt chose his words carefully. This quote conveys many critical ingredients to success in work and life:

"without the habits," "punctuality," "order," "diligence,"
"determination," and "concentrate on one subject at a time."

This book is written expressly for white-collar professionals,
executives, managers, and other personnel who are competent at their
professions but who have a hard time keeping up with the ever-
increasing demands being placed on them. Whether you work for a
large firm or have a small business to run, you must have proven
work habits and systems in place to successfully cope with these
increasing demands.

This book not only provides you with the proven processes and
systems, it also teaches how to use them. Not only will you do what
you do more efficiently and effectively, you will accomplish more of
what is most meaningful to you.

You, no doubt, are used to working hard. You know that
meaningful accomplishments do not come easily. If you wish to
increase your effectiveness you will have to work at it. In every
profession, there will be an expanding body of knowledge that is
critical to getting the job done right. Identifying and employing these
important pieces of knowledge is the most important thing you can do.

This book will help you to identify the most critical pieces of
knowledge necessary in the process of your personal work, to improve
your self-management, and to empower you to get the most results
for your efforts.

What do you get? More done. More control. Peace of mind. More
time. Less work. Easier time of it. Time to relax. Weekends with the
kids. Important goals accomplished. Better products. More satisfaction
with work. All of these things, and many more have been expressed
by those who have used the ideas in this book to improve how they
process their work.

How do they do that? Read on.

KERRY GLEESON

Boca Raton, Florida
August 1994

ACKNOWLEDGMENTS

My thanks go to the many people who directly and indirectly made this book possible.

To my Agent/Editors from Executive Excellence, Ken Shelton, Trent Price, and Meg McKay.

To John Mahaney, Senior Editor, Mary Daniello, Associate Managing Editor, and Gloria Fuzia, Editorial Assistant, at John Wiley & Sons.

To the staff at Crane Typesetting Service, Inc., for their management of the production.

To Kathryn Mikels, copy editor, Giorgetta McRee, designer, and Ralph Butler, illustrator, thank you.

To Dagfinn Lunde, John Birch, Frans Henrik Kockum, Kirk Stromberg, Mike Gallico, Rosaleen Hayes, Nancy Fredericks, and Mike Jurcy whose input vastly improved the book.

To Ira Chaleff, whose time and care made the book possible and whose concepts and words can be found throughout the manuscript.

To all of the Institute for Business Technology staff whose experiences and refinement of the PEP process have greatly enhanced its results and are the basis for this book.

To Lena Holmberg, Jay Hurwitz, Ron Hopkins, Eric Magnusson, Menno van der Haven, Peter Diurson, Johan Chr. Holst, Randi Bough

ACKNOWLEDGMENTS

Holst, Bruno Savoyat, Denis Healy, Ann Searles, and Tanya Seldomridge for all of their hard work and dedication.

To Jim Robinson, whose assistance with the development of the IBT software applications and techniques of organizing a computer were invaluable.

To Brita Norberg and Janita Thorner from Svenska Handelsbanken Sweden for giving me the opportunity to design the original Personal Efficiency Program.

To all of my many client friends who have taught me most of what you find in this book.

To my wife Jill for her love and my children Brooke, Mackenzie, and Quinn for the joy they bring.

To all of you, many thanks.

K.G.

CONTENTS

CONTENTS

CHAPTER 2

Organize It Now   31

CONTENTS

CONTENTS

CHAPTER 5

Follow Up and Follow Through   119

CONTENTS

CHAPTER 8

Maintain It Now   173

EPILOGUE

Just One New Habit   189

THE PERSONAL EFFICIENCY PROGRAM

INTRODUCTION

Personal Efficiency Program: The Missing Link

The obvious is that which is never seen until someone expresses it simply.
—KHALIL GHIBRAN

- Do you feel that you are always short of time?
- Do you feel that you have too much to do?
- Do you feel overwhelmed by everything you face at the office?
- Do you feel buried under mounds of paperwork most of the time?
- Would you like more time to do what you want?
- Do you often work overtime, into the evening, or on weekends to catch up on things you don't get done during working hours?
- Do you get stressed out because of what you don't get done?
- Are you unable to focus on the long-term improvement of your life and your work because you face continual crisis or overload?
- Do you wonder if you really are accomplishing what you want in your work and in your life?
- Would you like better results for the time and effort you invest in your work?
- Would you like to relax or vacation more often?

When asked these questions, most people answer with a resounding "yes." If your answer is also "yes," you're in for a pleasant surprise:

You can overcome these problems. You can accomplish what is most important to your work and to you and still find time for yourself, for your family, and for the things you'd like to do.

SOURCE OF THE PROBLEM

Why do people feel they never have enough time? Why do they feel both overworked and unproductive? The answer is quite simple. Although most of us have been formally educated to work in our professions, few of us, especially white-collar workers, have been taught *how* to work efficiently and effectively. Too many white-collar professionals have no idea how to organize themselves or how to best process their work. They may understand how to draw an architectural plan, write a clever ad, or negotiate a deal, but they can't effectively organize their week or cope well with interruptions and unexpected new opportunities and priorities.

A friend and coworker from the United Kingdom describes it this way:

You go to the university, get educated in your profession, and you get a job. You start your job, and all of a sudden the paper starts coming. No one ever mentioned the paper! What do you keep? Where do you put it? How do you find it again?

In my work I've met many bright and clever people who know their professions. They easily solve complex problems that boggle my mind. They build buildings, move cargo, develop products, sell services, even heal the sick. But for all their demonstrated capability and all their education, many of these people live stressful lives simply trying to keep up with all they must do. Why? Because, like you and me, these professionals were never taught the nuts and bolts of working in an office environment.

How you process your own personal work is just one example of a missing element in education. The Personal Efficiency Program (PEP) supplies the missing link.

I recently heard about a fascinating new program being tried at various universities around the country: The program is designed to teach professors how to teach. Imagine—teaching a teacher how to teach! Traditionally, professors haven't been trained in this one vital aspect of their profession: They are only required to demonstrate a conceptual mastery of their specialty. But as many university students could tell you, mastery of an academic discipline does not a great teacher make.

Parenting is another area that lacks basic training. How many couples receive any training in the fine art of parenting before they have children? Likewise few business managers receive any basic training in how to manage their own business!

HOW DO WE COPE?

Well, we're clever people. We know we could be more efficient and effective at work. How do we deal with this lack of education? We may see a colleague with some sort of organizer or calendar, so we get one. We learn from trial and error how to deal with our work as best we can. And most of the time we're pretty successful. We soon become comfortable with these tools. But, because the routines we establish to address our work are not necessarily based on the principles of work organization, they may not be as effective as they could be. The work habits we have may serve us well in one work environment, but when our job changes or the company merges or downsizes, it may take twice as much effort to achieve the same results. Our earlier ways of coping with the workload may not fit this new, more demanding work environment.

Because we are creatures of habit, even if we think a change in behavior would be good, making the change is always difficult. So what *are* the most effective ways of processing your work? How can you successfully change your behavior? How can you become more effective? These questions are answered in this book. And the book shows you how to address these issues efficiently. In the end you will work less, and it will be easier to do what you must do.

DOWN TO DETAILS

I once asked a very wealthy and successful man the secret of his success. He told me in two words: "Detail, detail." We all know our professional success comes from attention to detail, but we may not see how this attention to detail relates to how we personally work. The details of how to work have been defined in our PEP. The knowledge and experiences in this book come from the PEP process. Whether you modestly improve how you do your work or aggressively reengineer the whole process, you will be focused on the details of your work. By concentrating on these details, you will alter your behavior for the better. You will realize many more benefits than you can imagine.

Western manufacturing firms have spent a great deal of time and money analyzing, refining, and perfecting each step in the manufacturing process, especially since receiving their wake-up call from the competition. The effort shows. Productivity and quality have increased dramatically in manufacturing. But in white-collar work, from services to information processing to management, business processes are more difficult to analyze or reengineer. Personal work processes are rarely even considered part of the management business process, let alone analyzed and perfected.

NO LONGER A MISSING LINK

Because the knowledge of how to process your personal work to achieve both quality and quantity is missing in the white-collar world, we have a missing link in the quality and productivity chain, even in those companies that aggressively tackle these issues. Because it's missing, we often don't notice it: It's hard to see something that's missing. Still, this missing link is the cause of endless frustration for many white-collar workers in today's workplace.

PEP can supply that missing link in the productivity chain. It will help anyone who has a heavy workload. In the past ten years, PEP has helped 200,000 people get more done in the 168 hours of the week. PEP teaches you how to:

- Gain more control of your work.
- Make your job easier.
- Save time.
- Determine what is most important to you.
- Accomplish what is important to you.

PEP is a different way to process your own work that can multiply your personal productivity. I truly believe that it's possible for most people to double, if not triple, their current productivity, primarily because the vast majority of people don't produce all that much. This isn't to say people don't work hard. In fact, working with people in hundreds of companies and a dozen countries has taught me the opposite. People work very hard. And the vast majority of people want to do a good job. They try very hard to do exactly that. But most of us, for all of our hard work, just don't get all that much done. By working right, on the right things, there is hardly a limit to one's production capability. PEP provides the know-how to do things right and to work on the right things.

PEP will simplify your work. With it, you will exert less effort in work than you do now.

No matter what your motives are—whether you wish to become a millionaire or a couch potato, to get more done or to leave work on time—the fundamentals and basics covered in this book will help make those wishes happen.

This how-to book attempts to parallel the simplicity of the PEP program as it's delivered in person, one-on-one, by the one hundred or more trainers who work with the Institute for Business Technology. It's the codification of the experiences of those trainers, all of whom have succeeded in getting people to adopt better working habits. It's the input of 200,000 people on how they've developed systems, routines, and solutions that have allowed them to overcome their efficiency problems. All of this will help you get into a better working routine, which will, in turn, make you feel better about your performance and yourself.

It's one thing to have the information, another to act on it, and another still to change your behavior. There is no easy method to change, but we've developed tools that do work. When you completely purge your office, you'll recognize the principle: If you want to change your behavior, it's easier to do it completely. The concept of *Do It Now* will be drummed into you. It will both enable you to get more done and help you to overcome procrastination, a major block to behavioral change. You will begin to substitute good habits for bad. If we must be creatures of habit, let's at least make our habits good ones! Since our time and peace of mind are at stake, we ought to want to change.

PEP is like an exercise program: You have to do each step if you're to benefit. You can't just read about it. So if you don't plan to follow the program, don't read this book. Throw it away right now. Save yourself some time. Or follow the program, and save yourself a lot of time. The choice is yours. Personally, I hope you'll read the book. I hope you'll follow the program. I guarantee it will make a big difference in the quality of your life.

Do It Now!

*Those who make the worst use of their time are the first
to complain of its brevity.*
—JEAN DE LA BRUYÈRE

Chapter 1 Preview

In this chapter, you will learn how to:

- Get more done by doing it *now*.
- Overcome procrastination by getting in the habit of acting.
- Reduce your workload by doing the work once.
- Become more decisive by looking at the worst possible consequence of your action and then getting on with it if you can live with the consequence.
- Stop using priorities as an excuse not to do things.
- Start thinking. It is either important enough to do or it isn't; if it's important, then I'll act on it; if it's not important, I won't do it.
- Be as clever about completing things as you are about putting things off.

*N*ow! No doubt you hear the word all the time. If not from your boss, your spouse, or your child, you hear it from advertisers and salespeople. Some days it seems everyone and everything is demanding something now. A manager or coworker tells you someone didn't show up for work and what she was doing needs to be done by you, now. Or someone from home calls to tell you a pipe is leaking now. Or the telephone rings and demands to be picked up, now. An advertisement tells you to buy it, *now*. People and things demand our time and attention now, this moment, immediately. And so we find ourselves buried in our work, in spite of all the nice time management theories and tools.

Some time management gurus tell us we should ignore all the things that clamor for our urgent attention, including the telephone. They tell us we shouldn't react to circumstances and people around us; instead, we should organize, prioritize, and gain control of our lives by putting off some tasks and focusing our attention on those activities that are "most important," or "first things," or "top priorities."

Planning, setting goals, and priorities have a place. But too often, when we set priorities, we never seem to get around to everything on our lists. "Less important" activities get shoved into the closet by "more important" activities. Eventually, the "less important" things rot there. Not surprisingly, when they start to stink, they become very high priorities. And guess who has to clean up the mess? You do, of course, now!

WHY THE PERSONAL EFFICIENCY PROGRAM WORKS

The only method I've found that really produces the results people want—and the method you're going to learn here—is to gain the advantage by getting the "now" on your side. I call it the *Do It Now* approach to personal efficiency.

By *choosing* to *Do It Now*, you make *now* your ally, not your enemy. So, what do you do about the mess that accumulates on your desk? You *Do It Now*. Doing it now enables you to be better organized; to exercise greater control over the when, where, and how of what you're doing; and to feel better about yourself and your performance. Not surprisingly, *Do It Now* is the first tenet of the Personal Efficiency Program (PEP).

Does the following scenario sound familiar?

You arrive at the office, sit down, look at the papers spread out on your desk, and pick up one of them. It's from Mary. "Oh, I have to call Mary," you say. Dutifully, you start a To Do pile somewhere on your desk, and that paper goes into the pile. You pick up another piece of paper, this one a letter of complaint from a customer. You think, "I have to answer this letter." It goes on the To Do pile. The third piece of paper outlines a problem to be handled. "I have to talk to the boss about this," you mumble and onto the To Do pile it goes. You pick up the fourth piece of paper and say, "This isn't important. I can do it later." You create a Do Later stack next to your growing To Do pile, and so on. You end up shuffling through your various stacks of papers, and by the time you actually get back to your To Do pile and read through each piece again, you've wasted time reading everything twice. In effect, you've done the work twice, doubling your time commitment but accomplishing little.

This procedure would almost be okay if we only shuffled through paperwork twice, but some of us look at our papers three, four, or five times before we ever act on them. It takes a lot longer to do something four or five times than it does to do it once.

The first rule for improving personal efficiency is:

Act on an item the first time you touch it or read it.

I'm not talking about those things that you can't do now or even those things you shouldn't do now. I'm talking about all the things that you could and should do, but you don't. I'm talking about routine paperwork of the sort you encounter every day. Take care of these things the first time you touch them, and you'll save yourself a lot of time in the long run (and get rid of the paper!).

Call Mary. Respond to that E-mail message immediately. Answer the customer's letter of complaint. Act on that voice mail as you listen. Talk to the boss about the problem. *Do It Now.* You'll be amazed at how little time it actually takes and amazed at how good you feel when it's done.

If you're not going to act on your paperwork, don't waste time looking at it. If you're not going to return your voice mail messages, don't waste time listening to them. Don't clog up your day with things you *aren't* going to do. Instead, move on to what you *are* going to do, and *Do It Now*.

START WITH YOUR DESK OR WORK SPACE

When a person asks for my help in getting organized and putting the Personal Efficiency Program in place in their work and their life, the first thing I do is put them through a personal desk cleaning. I actually go to the person's desk and go through all their bits and pieces of paper with them. I'll pick up a paper and ask them what it is. They say, "Uh, well, that's something I was supposed to respond to."

"Okay," I say. Then they naturally start to put it somewhere, but I stop them. "Hold it a second. Why are you putting it over there?"

They give me an incredulous look and say, "Well, I have to do it, so I put it over there."

"Well, let's *Do It Now*."

"You want me to *Do It Now*? It could take some time . . ."

"I don't mind. I'll sit here while you do it."

And they do it. Usually, I clock it. And I say, "How long did that take?"

"One minute," they say, or "three minutes," or whatever.

"Look at that," I tell them. "See?"

"Yeah," they say, "it didn't take much time at all."

And I say, "I was hoping you'd notice that."

When this task is done the first time, it makes people uncomfortable. They do it, but they usually haven't grasped the concept yet, even though we talk about it and ask them to commit themselves to the concept and the work style. What they don't understand is that *Do It Now* is meant to be permanent and ongoing.

Even if they remember *Do It Now* and believe they follow the principle in the beginning, they are often inconsistent in their application of the *Do It Now* concept.

This is evident when I go back for a follow-up visit. Usually, they've cleaned up their office or work space in anticipation of my coming, with everything stacked neatly into piles. They're very proud they've mastered the concept. After all, it's easy enough to talk about *Do It Now* and even to get a person to agree with it. But most people think they *Do It Now* when they don't. Only by working with this concept consistently over time—as I do—do you begin to see more and more evidence of *not* acting the first time and all the reasons people make up for why they can't or shouldn't act now.

A first visit with one client included a thorough desk cleaning. We worked through every item on his desk, one at a time, until everything had been done that could be done. We talked about acting on things the first time—about doing it now—and he was so impressed that he committed himself to *Do It Now* as his new work philosophy.

When I went back for a follow-up visit, I hardly made it through the door before he started telling me that *Do It Now* was the greatest thing that had ever happened to him—it was just marvelous. He was very enthusiastic about the program and about the change it had made in his life.

Then I picked up the papers from his pending basket. The first piece of paper in it was a phone message. I said, "Why don't we call him now?"

He frowned just a little. "Now?" he said.

And I said, "Yes."

And so he picked up the phone and returned the call. By the end of our meeting, we'd gone through every single piece of paper in his pending basket.

Why was I able to empty his pending basket when he hadn't been able to? Because his definition of "pending" was something to be done later, and one visit with PEP obviously hadn't changed that.

Let me emphasize then. *Do It Now* means *Do It Now*, regularly and consistently, day after day. Not doing it now is what got you into trouble in the first place. Your pending basket is for things you *can't* do now, for things that are out of your control. For example, you call Mary back on Monday because that's when she's back from vacation, not because Monday seems like a good day to do it. *That's* pending.

Grasp the concept of *Do It Now* and the real meaning of "pending"—and function accordingly each and every day—and these simple words will literally change the way you approach your work and your life. You'll find yourself getting more work done than ever before.

OVERCOMING PROCRASTINATION

Simple procrastination probably eats up more time in the workplace than anything else. If you're a procrastinator, you'll find *Do It Now* is a key element in helping you to identify where procrastination exists in your work habits and helping you to overcome it.

Most people are very clever, even ingenious, about putting things off. "I don't have time" is a common excuse. "I think they said they're not going to be there today, so I didn't bother to call." "This could take forever, so I had better wait until I have a free day to start." "It's not so important." The list of reasons why a task can't be completed is endless.

My approach is this: *Be as clever about completing things as you've been about putting them off.* So Mary's not there. Who else could give you the information? Her assistant? Where else could you get this information? Who could this task be delegated to? How can you get this job done? That is the point, isn't it? How can you get that letter, that folder, or that report out of your in basket and off of your desk so that you never have to look at it again? That's where you should focus your brainpower—not on clever excuses.

This may sound simple, but it's a bitter pill to swallow: Too often the reason you're not getting things done is that you're just not doing them. You can reverse that trend, though, starting now—right now— by learning how to overcome procrastination and to increase your personal productivity. How? The following eight ways to overcome procrastination can benefit you immediately and immensely.

1. *Do It Once.* Sorting through all the papers on your desk and creating To Do and Do Later piles for yourself is a common practice. You have plenty of company if you're a pile creator. One woman I know goes through this creating piles process regularly. The first time through she calls it "reading for familiarity." The second read-through is her "action" read, unless she sets it aside "to do later." Now, this woman is a two-time cum laude graduate of a prestigious university, handling a responsible position in business! By adopting and implementing *Do It Now* she can immediately experience the most immediate benefit of PEP: *Do It Now*, and you do it once.

Needlessly rereading everything on your desk before acting on it achieves nothing. You know what's required the first time you read a customer's letter of complaint. Reading the letter twice only doubles your reading time and the letter is still not answered. Answer the letter the first time you read through it—*Do It Now*—and you save time, move toward customer satisfaction, and accomplish a task that, otherwise, prevents you from doing more important things.

2. *Clear Your Mind.* A client once described to me what it was like for him to drive home from work at the end of the day. When he would drive past a gas station, he would think: "I must get a spare tire for my car. I had a flat some time ago and have not gotten around to getting the spare." On he would drive and pass a pharmacy and think: "Vitamin C. We need Vitamin C. Winter is coming, and we need it for the expected sniffles." He would drive past a supermarket and think: "My wife wanted me to pick up bread. Ah, I don't feel like it." By the time he got home, he was exhausted. He told me he would be breathing hard. He needed a drink to calm down. "Everything I looked at reminded me of things I hadn't done!" he said. Mind you, not once did he stop and do any of those things. But he sure felt as if he had worked hard on these things. He was exhausted from procrastination.

Consider how many tasks and projects you have connected with your work. One hundred? Two hundred? Now consider how many tasks, incomplete activities, and wish-list items you have connected with your family. How many tasks or wish-list items could you list that are connected with your hobbies, your friends, civic, church, or other groups you belong to? As you add these up, you'll discover that the outstanding items—the things taking up space in your mind—probably number five hundred to one thousand.

Experience tells us that we're limited in how many tasks or activities our minds can juggle at any given time. How does this affect your work? Let's use the example of a customer's letter. You pick up the letter and look at the first line: "Can you please send me some information about a new product?" Immediately your attention flies off to the information you were supposed to send to someone else, but haven't gotten around to yet. You drag your attention back to the letter and read a bit further. "Can you meet with some of my colleagues to discuss a certain project?" Again your attention wanders off to several other meetings you need to prepare for but haven't gotten to yet. Once again you drag your attention back to the task at hand. The sheer volume of incomplete activities in your life distracts you from concentrating on and completing what's in front of you. This is where priorities fit into the picture.

Obviously, prioritizing can be an important part of controlling your work. But prioritizing can also be the best excuse *not* to do something. Prioritizing means that "unimportant" tasks get pushed off until later and may not ever get done at all. The consequence of not doing tasks in a timely way is your inability to focus on the work at hand because of the voices in your head reminding you of uncompleted tasks.

Have you ever made a list of ten things to do, only to have the bottom five never change? We tend to focus on top priority items and neglect lower priority items. That's why we call them lower priority, yet we still consider these things to be important.

My view is that things either should or should not be done. If deadlines are involved, certainly they must be considered, but if something is important enough to do, do it. Otherwise, don't.

The best way to eliminate task overload is to eliminate these little things that make you feel overloaded and pull your attention away from your major tasks. Act on these smaller, "less important" tasks. Make a list of all of them, set aside some quiet time and do them one by one. Or decide not to do one and trash it. Better yet, get yourself organized using the ideas in this book and don't allow tasks to accumulate in the first place.

With this overload eliminated, you're no longer distracted. Your level of concentration increases and, accordingly, you not only finish more tasks, you finish them better and more quickly than before. Komar was reported to have said:

Concentration, in its truest, unadulterated form, means being able to focus the mind on one single solitary thing.

If you can concentrate, focus, on what you are trying to do, you will bring to bear on the task one of the most critical elements of success.

3. *Solve Problems While They're Small.* As you gain experience in a job, you learn to detect those little red flags that tell you something is wrong and will only get worse if you don't take action. The question becomes: When and how do I act on these small indicators? Unfortunately, we tend to ignore these red flags too often in the face of more pressing issues.

Sometimes I point out a questionable stack of papers on the corner of someone's desk. Rather sheepishly, they admit, "It's my problem pile. I figure if they sit there long enough, they'll go away." And sometimes they do.

You've heard of Murphy's Law. In England it's called Sod's law: If anything can go wrong, it will. There's a corollary to Murphy's Law: If ten things can go wrong with something, you can be sure the one thing that will cause the most damage will be the one that goes wrong! Maybe most of those items in your problem pile will go away if you let them sit long enough. But you can be sure the one problem you don't want to happen will be the one that happens. And how much longer will it take you to take care of a crisis than the warning flag?

Get into the habit of acting on these things now, and you'll catch problems when they're still small, before they become big, time-consuming crises. As a result, you'll have more time to concentrate on the important things.

4. *Reduce Interruptions.* A common complaint I hear is about interruptions. Most people admit they have a hard time avoiding or preventing interruptions. Instead, interruptions are seen as something beyond the control of mortal men and the cause of nearly all our problems. How often have you heard or said, "Well, I would have gotten it done if I hadn't been interrupted every time I turned around!"

All too often, the interruptions people complain about are the result of their not having done something in the first place. As a result they not only have the work itself to do, but they also have to deal with those people who depended on that work being done, which only creates more work! Furthermore, most of us feel bad about having to explain why we haven't done something. Even if you have a perfectly good reason, and the person on the other end of the phone sympathizes with you, you'll be left with a bad taste in your mouth just because you had to beg off one more time with an excuse and an explanation.

If you want to avoid interruptions, do the tasks related to them. You can then spend more time on your work and less time explaining why you haven't done it. Gain a reputation for completing work on time, and you'll reduce interruptions further by eliminating those bothersome requests for interim project status reports.

Mind you, some interruptions are desirable. If a sale depends on immediate feedback, of course the sales manager wants to be "interrupted." Eliminating unnecessary interruptions and not aggravating the situation by creating reasons for others to interrupt you is what I'm referring to. Other benefits to eliminating these "self-created" interruptions are the improved quality of your work when you're free to concentrate on it fully and your ability to complete more work in the same amount of time because you're able to work undisturbed.

5. *Clean up Backlogs.* If you have to keep up with an ongoing heavy work flow and, at the same time, you have an accumulation of backlogs, you must address the backlogs if you're to get your work flow under control. Remember, backlogs create their own additional work, so eliminating them cuts down your workload more than you may imagine at first. There are five essential steps for handling backlogs:

1) Identify the backlogs.
2) Prioritize what backlogs to clean up first.
3) Schedule time each day to take a piece of the backlog and clean it up.
4) Identify the cause of the backlog.
5) Take steps to remedy the cause to prevent the backlog from happening again and to prevent any further buildup of backlogs.

Once we clear up old backlogs and prevent logjams from happening, we'll be better able to look to the future.

6. *Start Operating Toward the Future Instead of the Past.* Figure 1.1 illustrates what occurs mentally when you have lots of past due, incomplete, or old tasks yet to be done. The Xs on the diagram symbolize all of the tasks that should have been done then. Your focus is clouded by being dragged back into the past. Psychologists say that one indication of a person's mental health is the degree to which they operate in the past as opposed to operating in the present and future. Operating in or from the past is considered characteristic of a psychotic. Operating from the present toward the future is considered "sane." No wonder we can feel a bit "crazy" when we are overwhelmed with so many overdue tasks.

When you are operating in the past, you tend to focus on what might have been, on lost opportunities. Anything that directs you from the present toward the future is healthier than that which drags you back in time.

Suppose you are running a race in which the starting line is Present and the finish line is Future. If rather than starting the race at Present you start from the Past, you have that much more to run just to get to the starting line!

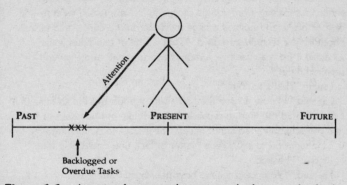

Figure 1.1. Attention focuses to the past, not the future, with a backlog of tasks.

7. *Stop Worrying About It.* It's one thing to waste time doing things over again or dealing with added interruptions or bigger "fires," but the real harm of putting things off is how it affects you mentally and emotionally.

Almost everyone tends to put off unpleasant tasks. A senior manager in an electronics firm in the United Kingdom put it this way: "Procrastination is the killer of time." Facing up to your unpleasant tasks and completing them isn't easy, but the consequences of *not* doing them can be much worse than simply dealing with the unpleasantness early.

To compound the problem, most people who procrastinate not only don't do the task, they also tend to dwell on the unfinished or undone task and worry about not having done it. This worry consumes far more time than people may realize. And it makes it harder to take causative action on it.

Think of some of the problems you've had to face in the past. Did dwelling on them get you anywhere? No. It was only when you finally initiated some action that the problem began to be resolved. If you face up to the big problems and unpleasant tasks and do something about them, they usually vanish rather quickly.

I once worked with a group of highly educated, bright, young service technicians from a large company in Denmark. I went to one of their desks and noticed a large machine on the corner and asked about it. The technician replied, "That's a bit of bad conscience. I received it from a customer a month ago to repair and I haven't repaired it yet."

I said, "That's terrible!"

He said "I know. I have thought about it a lot, but I'm so busy that I haven't had the time to repair it. It could take me two days to fix it, and my schedule is so tight I haven't been able to devote the time to it." He went on to say, "As a matter of fact, you could help me."

"How?" I asked.

He said, "You could tell my boss how busy I am."

Well, my help took a little different direction. I said, *"Do It Now."*

"I can't *Do It Now*," he argued. "I have a meeting at 2:00 o'clock, and. . . ."

"Okay. Just *Do It Now*, and let's see how far you get," I suggested.

Well, off he went into the repair area with the machine, muttering to himself. Fifteen minutes later he came back.

"Oh, no," I thought, "this could be trouble."

He looked at me and said, "It's done."

"Done?" I echoed.

"Yes, done," he said. "But it could have taken two days."

Of course, we don't always get so lucky. It could have taken two days to repair. But how often have similar things happened to all of us? When you finally get down to the business of doing something you've been putting off, it isn't nearly as bad as you thought it might be.

Most of us tend to exaggerate how long an unpleasant task will take or how unpleasant it really is. We dread doing it, so we put it off. Here was a man who had put off a job for a month, with the machine sitting there on his desk for a reminder of the thing he dreaded. He'd let it become a sore spot in his conscience and a sore spot between him and his boss. And rather than give the task the ten or fifteen minutes it actually required, he'd been blaming his boss for being too busy. In fact, of course, he'd been procrastinating, but regardless of the cause, the customer hadn't received service and had been without his machine for a month.

The trick? Face up to the unpleasant tasks and *act* on them *now*.

M. Scott Peck, in his book *The Road Less Travelled* (Simon & Schuster, 1978), called acting on unpleasant tasks "delayed gratification." Peck points out that life is difficult. People who procrastinate tend to want immediate gratification. Peck says:

> *Delaying gratification is a process of scheduling the pain and pleasure of life in such a way as to enhance the pleasure by meeting and experiencing the pain first and getting it over with. It is the only decent way to live.*

What tasks in your own work would you treat on a "worst-first" basis? Committing to a *Do It Now* mentality will help you overcome your resistance to dealing with unpleasant tasks. It will help you tackle the things you don't relish doing with a determination to have them over and done with. Some people take an almost perverse pride in being able to deal with the ugliest, meanest, most difficult things first. Most of us can improve our ability to handle the difficult head-on. Remember what Mark Twain said: "If you have to swallow two frogs, swallow the big one first, and don't look at it too long." So, if you can choose the sequence of your work each day, choose the task you enjoy least and do it first. Not only will the second task of the day be not quite so bad compared to the first, completing the worst first tends to give your self-confidence a boost.

8. *Now, Feel Better About Yourself.* Procrastination and attendant cover-ups, create a buildup of negative emotions not always evident on the surface. In one PEP course, a newly married lady began to laugh almost uncontrollably when the subject of procrastination was brought up. When asked what prompted this reaction she said:

> *Oh, I was thinking about my husband's ruffle shirt. You see I hate ironing, particularly my husband's shirt with the ruffle front. I would pull all the other items in the ironing basket out from under this shirt and do them first.*

When asked, "What happens when this shirt is the only thing left?" her response was, "Oh, I throw it back in the washing machine! My husband can't ever figure out where his favorite shirt has gone." A tremendous amount of emotional buildup comes with this habit of procrastination. It has strong impact on one's self-image.

By committing to *Do It Now*, completing the hard jobs first, and handling the big jobs bite-by-bite, you'll trim a tremendous load of stress and anxiety from your work. You'll gain more self-confidence and self-respect. Even after completing one day of the PEP program, participants have processed and purged all of the papers on and in their desk, in their computer, and their file drawers. They discover that they can accomplish much more than they ever realized before. They no longer have a guilty conscience. Almost instantly participants feel better about themselves.

> *Knowing when not to work hard is as important as knowing when to.*
> —HARVEY MACKAY, **Swim with the Sharks without Being Eaten Alive**

NOT EVERYTHING CAN OR SHOULD BE DONE NOW

Having said a lot about doing things now, let me point out that it isn't always possible or desirable to do everything now. You try to call Mary, but she won't be in until Monday. You're on your way to get coffee when a client calls about business. Clearly priorities do play an important part in productive work and in achieving results. However, ultimately success comes from getting things done. And too often people don't get things done because they don't do them! They do not *act, now*.

In fact, priorities can be the best excuse a person has not to do something. Yes, there will be times you can't *Do It Now*. There will be times you shouldn't *Do It Now*. Common sense is a necessity; it should be a given. The way to increase your personal efficiency is not to *Do Something Stupid Now*. If your approach toward work is to always choose, always prioritize, always give it some time to ripen, always have an excuse to look at it later, always shuffle through your papers or scan through your E-mail, you are *not* acting. In fact, you are reinforcing the habit of not acting. With *Do It Now* and no more excuses to procrastinate, the end product is a propensity to *act*.

BUILD DECISIVENESS INTO YOUR WORK HABITS

Successful people in general take little time to make a decision but take a long time to change a decision once it has been made.

Many people are afraid to be decisive. After all, if you make a decision, you have to live with the consequences. If decisiveness is a weak spot with you, there's an easy way to help you handle the quandary. Simply imagine the worst possible consequences of any decision you can make, and ask yourself if you can live with those consequences. If the answer is Yes, go for it.

You can't expect to be 100 percent certain of your course of action at all times. I understand, though, that George Patton, the famous World War II American general, worked with the following formula for success: "If you have a plan you're 80 percent certain of, you should violently execute it."

Then there is the Ben Franklin technique. Ben, the famous inventor, politician, and philosopher of the eighteenth century, had a method to help make decisions. Take a piece of paper and fold it in half. On one side, list all the reasons for making the decision. On the other side, list all the reasons against. By comparing these two lists, you can often get clarity on the direction you should go.

I've seen decisive people make the wrong decisions. Interestingly enough, they almost always made the intent of their decisions, that is, their objective, happen anyway. I believe there is some natural law connected with this phenomenon. The act of deciding may, in fact, be more important than the correctness of the actual decision and have more influence on the consequences. Be decisive, take action, and get on with your work and life.

ESTABLISH *DO IT NOW* WORK HABITS

Whether we like it or not, we're all creatures of habit. Most of us fall very easily into established routines. How often do you drive the same route to work, or eat at the same restaurant for lunch, or start each workday the same way, for example? Some of these habits and routines are good; others can work against us, and living totally by habit can be very destructive.

Are there habits worth cultivating? Certainly. Habits such as driving safely or showing courtesy to friends and colleagues should be routine and are definitely beneficial. Cultivating the *Do It Now* habit is intended to reinforce an action-oriented lifestyle; to become more decisive and to start and then to stay in motion. Many tasks we need to complete don't require a great deal of consideration and, yet, because that's our way of working, we treat them with the same weight that we assign to very important tasks with grave consequences. It's a habit. Your goal in reading this book is to break your old work habits and to become more efficient, and therefore more productive. Having a decisive and proactive approach toward work will enable you to do exactly that.

Procrastination is itself often only a bad habit.

In his book *Getting Things Done, The ABC's of Time Management* (Scribner's, 1976), Edwin Bliss describes procrastination as a habit in this way:

> *When we fail to act as promptly as we should it usually is not because the particular task in question is extremely difficult, but rather because we have formed a habit of procrastinating whenever possible. Procrastination is seldom related to a single item; it is usually an ingrained behavior pattern.*

I couldn't agree more. Learn to *Do It Now* and you'll short-circuit the habit of procrastination. *Do It Now* substitutes an action-oriented behavior for the "do it later" behavior. You act before the mental barriers are activated, so you don't have time to think "It's too hard; maybe it will go away; I'm not in the mood; maybe someone else will see it; I don't feel like it."

DISCIPLINE

A common word heard when discussing the subject of changing behavior is discipline. "It is a matter of discipline. If I had more of it, I would be able to exercise, . . . stop smoking, . . . diet . . ." While discipline plays a part, I believe it is a red herring. If you exert discipline enough to establish a routine, you make a new habit. The habit helps you maintain it. Discipline yourself to act now, and it will very soon become a habit. Then the habit will lessen the need for discipline. William James, whose studies of human behavior are well known, suggests that if you do something every day for thirty days, it will become a habit. Try it with *Do It Now*.

To be honest, this is more than dealing with procrastination. It is a philosophy toward work and life. It is the view: I am proactive; I am action-oriented; I am bigger than the problems I face. These characteristics begin (and end) with how you face up to and habitually act on the small details of work and life.

So, what is the first thing you should Do Now? Go ahead—write it down. Focus on the first things. Get yourself organized to *Do It Now*, and do it better!

FOLLOW-UP FOR CHAPTER 1

1. Get started. Go to your desk—if need be, with this book in hand—and go through every single bit and piece of paper on your desk or anywhere near your working space. Pick up the first piece of paper and determine what it is and what must be done to process it to completion. Do whatever is required to complete that task and get that piece of paper off your desk so you never have to look at it again. If a task is going to take you several hours to complete, schedule a time to do it.

2. Determine what tasks ought to be done and decide what must be done to process each task to completion. Take the task as far as you possibly can. If you run into a roadblock, get clever. Ask, "How can I get this done another way?" If you decide to delegate the task or pass it on to someone else, remind yourself to follow up.

3. Stop shuffling endlessly through the same materials over and over. Eliminate To Do piles and To Do Later piles. Act on an item the first time you lay your hands on it.

4. Redefine the word "pending." Pending does not mean something to do later. *Do It Now* means *Do It Now*, regularly and consistently, day after day. Your Pending box is for things you can't do now, not for things you don't want to do now. If you don't have the time to do something the first time you set hands on it—a report that will take three hours to write, for example—schedule time for the report, file it so it doesn't get lost, and move on promptly to the next item. You'll return to the report at the appropriate time.

5. Stop procrastinating. Procrastination eats up more time in the workplace than practically anything else. *Do It Now* is a key element in helping you to identify where procrastination exists in your work habits and helping you to overcome it. The trick is to be as clever about completing work as you've been about avoiding it. Do it once; clear your mind of clutter; solve problems while they're small; reduce interruptions; clean up backlogs; stop worrying about it; feel better about yourself; do the worst first; and be decisive.

You can overcome procrastination and get out from under if you establish good *Do It Now* working habits.

CHAPTER 2
Organize It Now

**4S—A Japanese management strategy to increase quality
and improve personal effectiveness.**

SEI-LI	*Organization*
SEI-TON	*Orderliness*
SEI-KEZ	*Neatness*
SEI-SOU	*Cleanliness*

Chapter 2 Preview

In this chapter, you will learn how to:

- Clean up your act and save yourself time.
- Stop wasting your time looking for things. Set up separate file systems for your working papers, reference papers, and archive papers.
- Organize your computer files and set up proper directories for computer files and E-mail.
- Put as much attention to detail in how you are set up to work as you do on the work itself.

You must be well organized to establish the routines that allow you to develop the *Do It Now* habit. You'll be surprised at the time you save just by organizing your work area for maximum efficiency.

A SOLDIER'S STORY

A soldier is a study in attention to detail. When recruits arrive for basic training at boot camp, they are drilled in what some may consider very fundamental skills. Apart from a tough physical regimen, soldiers are taught in the most forceful way how to make their bed, how to polish their shoes, how to organize their toiletries, how to clean and maintain their weapons, and other fundamentals. The sergeant, no doubt, wants to impress upon them the need to follow orders. But it is more than that. Basic training in the armed service is just that—basic. Attention to the basics constitutes the foundation for a successful soldier.

There is no more serious profession than that of a soldier, especially during war when their lives are on the line. Considerable thought is put into where a weapon is placed on the body. Soldiers are trained to keep their weapons in meticulous condition. When an enemy is approaching the soldier can't afford to have his gun jam because it wasn't kept clean. An undisciplined, disorganized soldier who doesn't know where his weapons are and who takes no care of them will soon be a dead soldier. That's why sergeants are deadly serious about teaching these basics to new recruits.

During the Gulf War, I was fascinated to watch a television interview of the highest ranking officer of the ground division. When asked about its successful engagement, he said "Yes, all of the equipment arrived on time and was placed where it belonged."

How well you are prepared and organized for your work is far more serious than most people recognize. Clutter can be a killer.

CLEANING OUT THE CLUTTER

Clutter is the mess you face every day when you walk into your office. It's your coat flung over the back of your office guest chair because you didn't hang it on the coat tree that morning. It's the half dozen reports perched on the corner of your filing cabinet and buried under the remains of yesterday's in-office lunch. It's the stack of magazines you haven't gotten around to reading yet. It's the mound of outgoing and incoming mail strewn across your desk. It's the unfinished letters you are writing by hand to give them a personal touch. It's the cassette tapes you meant to take home to listen to over the weekend but are now buried under the quarterly budget.

Clutter is the excessive disorganized mess you don't need in your working environment. We may yell at the kids every day to clean up their rooms and then go to a messy office and never even notice anything wrong. But clutter in an office and desk environment prevents us from effectively doing our work.

WHERE DOES CLUTTER COME FROM?

The first culprit is paper. Whatever happened to the idea of a paperless office? At one time, people speculated that technology would produce an office free of the clutter of paper because everything would be electronic. That still may happen, but it hasn't happened yet. The computer prints out more paper than we can get rid of, and copy machines churn out reams of paper very efficiently. In fact, the flow of paper is probably worse now than it ever was.

E-mail may even be worse than paper clutter, if that's possible. Although E-mail is a wonderful invention, it has created electronic clutter. You can now send a memo to 150 people with a single keystroke. Some people are getting up to two hundred E-mail messages a day on a full system. Can you imagine? Or maybe you don't have to. If your office is "fully computerized," you may not have to imagine it at all.

The deluge of information coming into the office is another source of clutter. Then there's how we look at the subject. A friend just cleaned out his clothes closet. His wife forced him to do it; she suspected mice were nesting in there. Offices are like clothes closets— places where we accumulate a lot of stuff. The same man and his wife moved across the street to a new home and took all that stuff with them. Much of what they moved they had stored months and even years ago, knowing someday they were going to need it. And they put it all in the storage closet in their new house and haven't been in there for months.

We laugh about such stories, but that's normal. Most people think it is possible they will need all the stuff they keep. Everybody keeps their *National Geographic* magazines, but they never look at them. So why keep them? Why keep them organized? It's like a soldier who would love to carry a tank into battle with him but that's just not possible. At some point you have to look realistically at what you're carrying around and make sure you're carrying around things you actually need. If not, get rid of it!

WHY CLUTTER STAYS THERE

Clutter represents the way people approach both work and life. It tells something about those people—they may have a cluttered mind as well. Many people justify clutter by saying it gives them food for thought and adds to the creative process. Others believe creative and artistic people are just born this way. A colleague of mine once told an interesting story. She described the first time she went to a famous artist's home in New York. Before she went, she had an image in her mind of what a real artist's home would look like: avant-garde, very messy, with paintings stacked in the corners, the studio filled with things to stimulate the creative juices.

But when she walked into his house and looked around, she found that it was neat and tidy. She thought perhaps he'd straightened up since he was expecting guests, but when she found her way into his studio during the evening, she saw that the studio, too, was in perfect order. All the paint brushes were exactly in order, and the paint cans were neatly lined up and labeled. She could hardly believe what she was seeing—it violated her expectations of how an artist works.

When she asked him about his neatness, he said he had learned it in college, when he had studied art. He had been taught to keep his tools in good working order. He knew that paint brushes would be ruined unless cleaned after each use. He labeled all the different kinds of paint, because if he didn't, he knew that he'd forget what colors he'd mixed.

If you want to operate effectively, like this artist, you must have things operational and organized. It's simply easier to function in a clean and neat environment.

OUT OF SIGHT?

I know people who fear out of sight literally means out of mind. They're afraid they'll forget about a task or an assignment if they don't have some physical reminder of it on their desk or Post-it™ notes stuck in sight. Keeping everything in sight is their solution.

I agree. Out of sight very often does mean out of mind. When people tell me they have trouble remembering things, I give them a system to remind them. Furthermore, they don't need to be reminded of all the things on the desk that they can't do anything about. Being reminded of what you can't do now only reinforces the bad habit of *Do It Later.*

Start organizing yourself by cleaning up. Get rid of the clutter. Separate the useful tools from the useless. Decide what to keep and what to get rid of. Clean it up, and at the same time put in systems and routines to prevent clutter from building up again.

DON'T OVERLOOK THE OBVIOUS

Very often we overlook the obvious in trying to improve the work process. We try to solve more complex problems and miss the fundamentals. The fundamentals a white-collar worker deals with every day include his or her desk, staples, pens, tape, paper clips, lights, chair, computer, file systems, binders, computer disks, and much more. It's not uncommon to walk into an office and find these items in disarray—scissors misplaced, staplers broken, tape dispenser empty, papers scattered randomly. Yet somehow we expect to work effectively in this condition.

Many people never realize that by not having the basics of their own workplace in order, they handicap themselves from dealing effectively with their day-to-day problems.

Trivial? Maybe, but the *Wall Street Journal* once reported that white-collar workers spend an average of six weeks a year looking for things in the office! Incredible? Yes, but in my experience, true.

I once visited a high-ranking bank executive who was responsible for a region employing 2,500 people. He was a clever businessman who had risen through the ranks due to his leadership ability and business sense. He was very overloaded and wanted my help sorting it out. One day I noticed a stack of paper on his desk and asked about it. He said it needed to be hole-punched, but he hadn't gotten to it yet. I could have questioned, why was he doing it in the first place, but I decided to teach him a lesson on *Do It Now*, and so I asked him to hole-punch it now. He said, "sure," and proceeded to leave the office. I followed him out past his assistants, down the hall, through a door, down a flight of stairs and into a supply closet. He took a hole-puncher and walked back to his office and proceeded to punch the holes. Each time he would need to put holes in the paper, he went through this process. I asked, why not get your own hole-puncher? He looked at me and said, "What a good idea." He had simply never thought of it.

The obvious isn't only access to the tools you use. Step back and take a good look at your office environment. Is your desk set up most suitably? Is your office warm enough in winter and cool enough in summer? Is your chair comfortable?

Once I did a personal efficiency program (PEP) for Philips Electronics. While visiting one participant's office, I noticed he was very uncomfortable, just sitting there, squirming. I asked what the problem was, and he said, "My back hurts."

I examined his chair and saw that it was broken. So I said, "Why don't you get a new chair?"

When I went back for a follow-up visit, he had a new chair. He said, "This is pretty amazing. I got a new chair and my back pain went away. I'm doing so much better at work just because of my new chair."

Another man increased his productivity dramatically simply by having his desk face the window instead of the door. Because the door was open all the time, people would walk by and distract him or make eye contact. If he made eye contact, people felt they could stop, come in and say hello, and spend time visiting. As a result, he was constantly interrupted. When he turned his desk and chair so they faced the opposite wall, people stopped interrupting his work.

Entire new sciences are being built up around the idea of examining and improving how people interact with their surroundings. The Digital Equipment Corporation (DEC) is promoting a concept in Sweden it calls the office of the future. Everything is taken into consideration, from the kind of hardware and software used to the color of the walls. It has examined the types of furniture that provide the best back support and subtle production support that comes from being in a comfortable environment.

DEC has even considered how cultural differences influence the definition of a comfortable environment. For example, in Sweden the office of the future looks like a Swedish country home. Why? Because people felt they could be more productive in the environment of a Swedish country home rather than a plain office. The lesson to be learned here is this: If you want to improve your work performance, you need to ensure that your tools are in good working order and that your work environment is conducive to productivity.

To be more competitive, many companies have had to give specific attention to the production process. Machines are designed specifically to perform certain operations; sometimes the product itself is redesigned to facilitate efficiency; and people are trained not only in how to use the equipment, but in how to use their ingenuity to make the process more effective. Unfortunately, for the most part, this attention to detail hasn't yet found its way into the white-collar arena.

Part of the problem is that most white-collar work can't be quantified and measured as easily as producing pens on an assembly line. Still, the principles remain the same. Recent progress has been made because quality gurus like W. Edwards Deming, Philip Crosby, and others have made people take a closer look at how they work. Reengineering, a more radical revamping of the work process than simple process improvement, is the current rage. But even when looking at how the work processes evolved or how they may be reengineered, quite often we're still not starting with the basics. We must look at the systems and routines employed in our work and apply them to the work that must be done, then step even further back and look at the personal work environment and the personal tools we use to accomplish tasks.

> *I invent nothing, I rediscover.*
> **—AUGUSTE RODIN**

START WITH THE BASICS

If you want to organize yourself for greater productivity, you must consider some very basic ideas most people never master. Are your tools operational? Is your product easy to produce? These are two of the questions white-collar workers need to ask themselves, although they rarely do.

On an assembly line, if a worker has to bend over and pick up a heavy tool each time he puts a tire on a car, the process needs redesigning. Maybe the worker needs a leverage device of some sort to lessen the time and effort required to put on the tire. Similarly, if you have to rummage through several different papers or directories every time you need to make a phone call, you need to redesign the process. The idea is to make it easy to *Do It Now*.

YOUR OFFICE TOOLBOX

Let's get specific about the tools you use in your work. If you're not reading this chapter at your desk, imagine yourself there. Think about the physical layout of your work space. What items are there?

Three Trays. First there should be in, pending, and out baskets or trays for your day-to-day paper flow (not for storage!). Your tray system should look as shown in Figure 2.1.

Standard Office Supplies. Then there are the things you use every working day: stapler, pens, pencils, tape, business card holder, maybe a pencil sharpener, calculator, paper clips, formatted disks, and so forth—all the tools of white-collar work.

I occasionally meet people who have two or three "broken" staplers in or on their desks. They're not really broken, of course—they're just jammed, usually because the staples are stuck in the mechanism and no one got around to unsticking them. Worse, each time a stapler was needed they would borrow one! As insignificant as a stapler may seem, it's a basic tool for a white-collar professional, and having this and other fundamentals in place allows you to work in the most efficient and effective manner.

Make sure that you have all the tools you need and that all of your tools are operational. No more borrowing a pair of scissors or a stapler every time you need one. Take the time to look at all the tools you have or should have. At the end of this little exercise, you will have a stapler, pens, pencils, a pencil sharpener, pads of paper, cellophane tape, business card holder, paper clips, formatted disks, files, file labels, and whatever other items you normally use in the course of a

THE TRAY SYSTEM

IN, PENDING, AND OUT TRAYS MUST BE WITHIN ARM'S REACH FOR EFFICIENCY

Incoming Mail and Notes. Never before touched. When you pick something up, act on it! If you have a secretary, mail should be screened and sorted into folders that suggest priority when you are rushed (for example, signature, Urgent, memos, reading).

Short-term pending, 24–48 hours. For things you have tried to act on and couldn't complete (e.g., awaiting info, awaiting call-back, interrupted for more urgent matter).
Not for: Procrastination
         Incomplete projects
         Tickler items

Collects completed items for removal. Remove several times a day when leaving office or have secretary do so.

Optional, if you have a lot of reading material. Prevent buildup by reading short items at once, scanning table of contents and clipping articles, sharing reading load across department and clipping or summarizing, scheduling a time for regular reading.

Figure 2.1. The tray system.

day, and they will all be fully functional. These routine items should be stored in the middle drawer of your desk or in the shallower side drawers of the desk—not on your work surface.

At the same time, be alert to waste. I often hear stories of incredible waste from the accounting departments of companies. People say, "Once we got organized, we found what we had in inventory, what we were using and wasting." When calculated the amount of waste often boggles the mind.

I once taught PEP to a medium-size brokerage firm. I started going through desks one by one. I told them, "Make sure to gather up any extra supplies you have, so they can be returned to central supply." I do this because people often complain that they go to central supply but can't find what they need or, in small companies, that the supply budget has been spent for the quarter or the year, and there's no money to buy additional supplies. Well, as I went through PEP with about 120 people in the company, I rounded up all the extra supplies people had in their desks. In the end they had enough supplies to last them a year without buying a single thing! All they had to do was organize what we'd retrieved from everyone's desks. And that's typical. If you're up to the challenge, look in, on, and around your own desk. I bet you'll find half a dozen extra pens and other supplies you didn't even know you had.

The same principle that applies to supplies in your desk also applies to information in your files: *You don't use what you don't realize you have.* And without organization and maintenance, you don't realize what you have. You're wasting resources. Think of the survivors of a shipwreck, on the ocean in a rubber raft. The first thing they have to do is account, item by item, for every resource available to them so nothing is wasted. Waste in such a situation could cost them their lives.

Photocopiers. Another tool millions of workers use Monday through Friday is the office photocopier. I know this sounds petty, but not knowing how to make a copy can cost plenty. A friend of mine once told me this story. He had traveled to California to consult with a client. He was meeting with the CEO and president in the conference room. After my friend presented his one-page overview, the CEO wanted a copy made. The CEO stopped the presentation, called in a copy specialist and then waited. Twenty minutes later the copy specialist came back with a single piece of paper. Later, just out of curiosity, my friend asked why it took so long to get one copy made. An assistant to the CEO took him down a long hall, through several doors, and finally into the copy room. There was a huge copy machine—a monster with many gadgets and dials and dozens of bins for everything. You could launch the space shuttle from that room as easily as you could make a photocopy. Approximately 90 percent of the office staff didn't know how to use it.

Fax Machines. You should also know how to use a fax machine, how to use a printer, and all the other tools used in common by staff. The machines should be operational and stocked with supplies and replacement parts. Simple instructions on how to use the machine should be posted. And you should take the time to familiarize yourself with them.

Computers. Sometimes people use their computing tools properly but not to the fullest extent possible. An example would be using a computer to do only one spreadsheet activity and ignoring functions such as word processing, invoicing, tracking, and calendar work. A computer can be used in many ways, but most people only learn one function. With some computers, you can send and receive faxes directly through the computer. You can do your banking, pay your bills, and order theater tickets through the computer without ever leaving the office or mailing a thing. When we work with large corporate clients, we often find that half the staff does not know how to use many of the basic features of their own E-mail system, installed to improve their productivity. Using the full capabilities of the computing tools available to us is important. Perhaps even more important is continual working to find new ways to use those tools.

STAY FAMILIAR WITH TOOLS AS THEY COME ON THE MARKET

Become familiar with the best time management systems and tools. Make a habit of browsing through catalogs or at an office supply store periodically to discover new resources and tools.

I recall one woman who worked for an insurance company. She was very disorganized and didn't want to follow my suggestions. Truthfully I felt she was pretty hopeless. But then one day a colleague brought in a time management system that had three-by-five cards and a leather binder with little sleeves to hold the cards. The system required users to write a task on each card; if users don't complete the task, they slip the card into a sleeve for the next day. Well, her colleague found this system useless and was about to throw it away. Instead, she gave it to this woman who loved it and ended up solving many problems by using it.

Many excellent tools can be employed to increase both your effectiveness and efficiency. One person may find one tool ineffective whereas another person can't live without it. Take advantage of the tools that exist and find tools that are suited to your style and personality.

FILING SYSTEMS AND PAPER CONTROL POINTS

To deal better with paperwork, organize your papers and files by frequency of use. The things you use most frequently need to be near at hand. Your desk is a work surface, and the only papers on it should be those you are working with currently.

Figure 2.2, showing paper control points, gives an overview of good office organization.

You should have a three-basket system for handling paper flow. Your in, pending, and out baskets (trays) are for tasks completed over the course of a few days at best. Next set up three types of files: working files, reference files, and archive files. These three files are vital paper control points for managing your work flow.

Working files are for current projects and routine functions. Usually 80 percent of your work involves 20 percent of your files, so these files should be kept within arm's reach, most likely in your desk drawers as hanging files. Working files are for items you're concerned with regularly over several weeks or months and for ongoing projects you're responsible for.

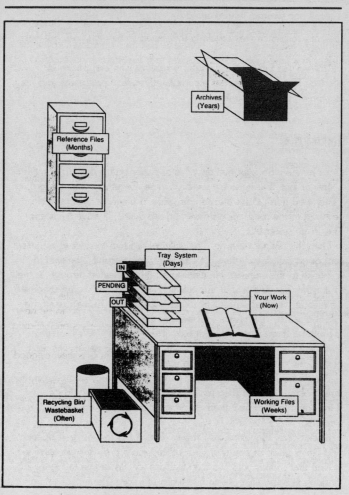

Figure 2.2. Paper control points.

Reference files contain the bulk of the files in your office. Since you use your reference files regularly they need to be near you, but not necessarily within arm's reach.

Archive files are kept for statutory reasons and may rarely be needed. They represent the accumulated work of past years and may be stored outside the office.

Working Files

Once a man who kept five tall piles of paper on his desk told me with a straight face that he knew exactly where everything was. I asked, "Then you don't think there's any value in having a system?" He gestured to the mess on his desk and answered: "I have a system. This is my system."

Then the telephone rang. The caller asked him to refer to a memo sent out a few days before. "Yeah, sure, one second," he said in response to this request. He went to a pile and leafed through it; then to another pile and leafed through it; then he looked at me sheepishly, his face turning red, and went to yet another pile. Embarrassed, he told the caller, "I'll have to get back to you."

I just sat there and looked at him. Then he said: "Well, maybe there is a need for PEP, but honestly, that missing paper was right next to the blue piece of paper in that folder."

People think they know where things are, but they waste precious time looking because they really don't know. And it would be unreasonable to expect them to remember where every single piece of paper is.

If your boss suggested you should remember the location of each and every piece of paper in your office, you'd probably be outraged.

And that's what your working files are for. As shown in Figure 2.3, working files usually contain five types of information:

1. *Fingertip Information.* These files contain phone lists, address lists, computer codes, company policies, and other information you refer to frequently and want at your fingertips when you need it.

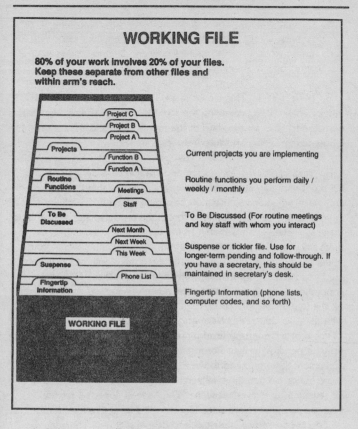

Figure 2.3. Working files.

2. *Items "To Be Discussed."* Create a file for routine meetings and a file for each staff member with whom you interact.

3. *Routine Functions.* These files contain information that you need for routine tasks performed daily, weekly, or monthly.

4. *Current Projects*. These are the projects you're working on now. Create a hang file for each project and include anything necessary for your current work. Clean these files now and then to move certain less urgent items to reference files.

5. *A Tickler File*. This file is usually divided in two parts: one is numbered 1–12, representing the months of the year; the other part is numbered 1–31, for the days of the month. The tickler file is used for longer-term pending and follow-through items.

By creating a tickler file system and checking it daily, you have a fail-proof reminder system. For example, suppose that I'm your client and we're scheduled to meet on December fifteenth. There are notes in your tickler file to remind you to call me on December thirteenth to make sure everything is ready. In the file folder for the thirteenth there's also a note to confirm all of our appointments. Also in your tickler file at appropriate points throughout the month of December are items such as "Verify flight schedule" and "Check Chicago connection," along with a note reminding you to brief your assistant on the Lyman account so she can substitute for you in the meeting with them scheduled for December fifteenth.

The tickler file can be used for storage in a way that avoids clogging up your pending basket. For instance, suppose you have an agreement that you need to write, and you know it's going to take some hours. So you have all sorts of papers—perhaps a first draft to be rewritten by a given deadline. You haven't done this rewrite because you know from experience it will take at least two hours, and you don't have a two-hour block to devote to it until Thursday. So you block out two hours on Thursday's calendar, and you place the rough report in the tickler file for the eleventh, where you know you'll find it when you're ready to get down to work. Then, because it's your habit to check the tickler file each morning, on the eleventh you locate the rough draft in your file and check your calendar. Sure enough, you've blocked out time between 9 and 11 A.M. to work on the report. And when the final draft is completed, you'll place it into your out basket and route it to the next person involved.

Everything I am referring to in a paper tickler system equally applies to an electronic tickler system. It can be a specific personal information manager (PIM) software. Or a Wizard-type handheld organizer. Such electronic tickler systems often exist as part of an E-mail system. For those of us without administrative support, electronic systems are often more effective and easier to use than paper-based systems.

You can see why it's essential to check the tickler file daily. This is the essence of the *Do It Now* philosophy. After checking the tickler file for the day, you know exactly what you must do to keep on schedule and accomplish the tasks that will move you further along in your work.

As you set up your own working files, follow these guidelines:

1. *Select your working file drawer*, most likely one of your larger desk drawers. Remember, this is information you want close at hand. Label the drawer appropriately and clearly in big, bold letters.

2. *Remove all nonworking files.* Move them either to reference files or archive files.

3. *Make sure you have a file folder for each project and activity.* Label each file appropriately and clearly.

4. *Set up a tickler file.* One part is numbered 1–12, representing the months of the year; the other part of the tickler file is numbered 1–31, for the days of the month.

5. *Remove files that are no longer active.* Move either to reference files or archive files.

Reference Files

You're now going to create your own reference files. Your reference files will contain these items:

- Research for your future projects.
- Past projects to which you refer.

- Resource information.
- Personnel information.
- Administrative data.
- Budget information.
- Client account records.

As you set up your reference files, consider these two things:

- What information do you want to retain?
- How can you best organize your reference files for ease of retrieval?

For many people, throwing things away is difficult. Just how much information should you retain? Consider the following:

- Do you tend to hold onto things "just in case?"
- Do you keep too much in your reference files?
- When deciding whether to save something, take Stephanie Winston's advice from her book *Getting Organized* (Norton and Company, 1978) and ask yourself, "If I needed this again, where can I get it?"
- Can someone else in the organization provide the information? If so, don't duplicate his or her files unless you use this information frequently.
- Do you need to coordinate with anyone to determine who will save certain pieces of information?
- Do you need to coordinate with anyone with whom you share reference files on how you will organize files?

The following ideas might help you to structure your reference files (see Figure 2.4):

1. List the key components of your job (for example, contracts, trade fairs, product development, budget, personnel). These will become the categories in your reference files.

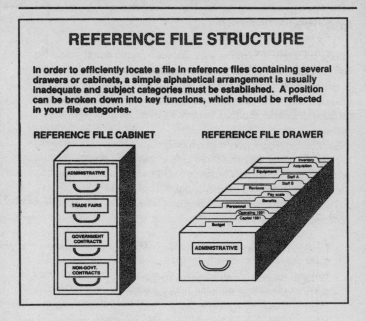

Figure 2.4. Reference file structure.

2. Label file folders clearly and appropriately, based on the categories you identified.

3. Cull existing files and throw away useless paper.

4. Using hanging files, organize drawers with one or more categories.

5. Alphabetize files within categories or subcategories.

6. Label file drawers and file folders with large, clear letters to make retrieval and refiling easier and faster.

Archive Files

At one company, I found in a file drawer a memo dated 1906. No one had gone through those files since 1906! The memo was on how to clean the office. True. One of our PEP consultants carried a little case with screwdrivers and a hammer because it was so common to go into offices and find that he couldn't even open some of the cabinets.

Staff members are generally reluctant to use the archive system because they feel they can't trust it. Management's responsibility is to provide a functional archive system; staff's responsibility is to understand the archive system and use it correctly.

The following questions will give you an indication of the state of your archive file system:

- Do you have departmental archives? What about company archives?
- What is the policy on document retention?
- Who is responsible for maintaining archives?
- Does an indexing system exist?
- What are the procedures for retrieving documents from archives?
- Can you rely on documents being recovered if needed?
- Have you tested this system lately?
- Do archive files need to be implemented? If so, who should do this?

TIPS FOR IMPROVING YOUR FILING SYSTEM

The following suggestions (see also Figure 2.5) will make your filing system more efficient:

- Use hanging files. Hanging files support files better and facilitate refiling in the correct place. Box-bottom hanging files can hold several manila files on the same subject.

- Label files with large, clear letters. This facilitates retrieval and refiling.
- Align category and subcategory labels. Aligning the tabs according to categories and subcategories allows the eye to more efficiently scan to the correct file. Categories can be given colored labels to further aid scanning. (Make sure this step is necessary and useful.

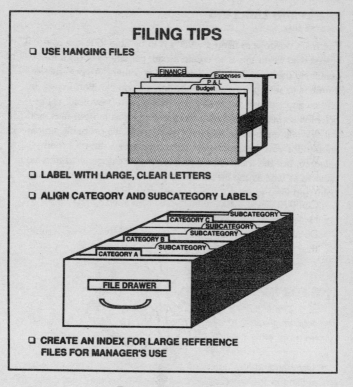

Figure 2.5. Filing tips.

I was told of one secretary who spent an entire day color coding her supervisor's files only to discover he was color blind.)

• Create an index for large reference files. This index enables anyone to retrieve files easily in the secretary's absence. It also minimizes duplicate files and coordinates the use of shared files.

FILING AND LABELING

The main purpose in filing anything is to be able to find it again. The easiest way to do this is to create broad, general categories that will be genuinely useful and easily understood by others. A good rule of thumb is to set up file systems not only so you can find things, but also so anyone else can find them. The reason is twofold: (1) on occasion somebody else may need to find items in your files, and (2) if it's simple enough for someone else to use, it's probably simple enough for you. You can always subcategorize within a broad category, but the main idea is to have bigger categories. Label your drawers as well as the files within them, using lettering that is big, bold, and easy to read.

ELECTRONIC FILES

With changes in technology, paper isn't the only thing you need to control and organize within your office and your system for work. You also have the computer.

Not too long ago, trying to organize the files on a PC's hard drive was next to impossible. Yes, utilities exist to help organize the PC files. But these applications were, themselves, misunderstood and difficult to operate. Fortunately, operating systems like OS/2 and applications such as Windows have made the process easier.

A computer is much like an empty filing cabinet. You can dump your applications and data files into it in a pile, or you can group your applications and files, set up general categories, divide them into drawers and subcategorize the files in these drawers, much as you would with your paper files. (See Figure 2.6.) It is possible, and desirable, to organize the hard drive, the desktop (a term used in OS/2 and Windows describing the background where the graphic symbols called objects or icons reside), menus (the list of options and or instructions to be found by clicking on an icon or object) and files (electronic documents that have been given a name and stored on your computer).

Depending on the operating system and software applications in your computer, you can establish general categories on the hard drive, such as Graphics for any and all desktop publishing applications you have, Word Processing for your word processing applications, Database for database applications, Utilities for all utility applications, Operating Systems should you have more than one, or PIMs for any personal calendaring/organizing software you may have.

With Windows or OS/2 (Figure 2.7) you can easily organize your desktop objects or icons to match your organization of the hard drive. When you wish to get into your database application and database files you need only double click your mouse on the object or icon representing the database applications and a window pops up on the screen listing the different database applications you can choose from.

You should organize your computer so software applications are

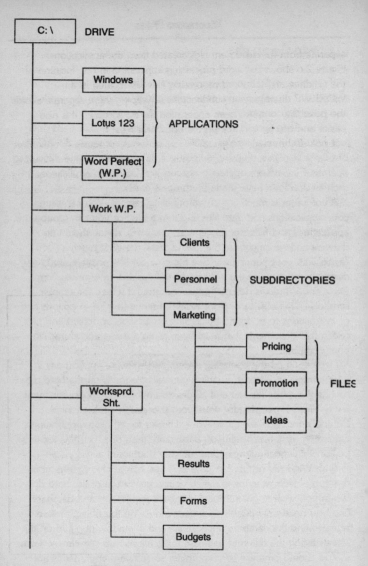

Figure 2.6. Computer directories.

separate from the document files created from the applications. Figure 2.6 shows the word processing application in one location of the C: drive and the word processing files are located in the WORKWP directory and subdirectories. Keeping them separate avoids the possibility of deleting an application file by accident. It is also easier and quicker to back up the document files.

Look at the paper working files you set up. A directory (a collection of files and/or other directories, called subdirectories, that are stored at the same location on a disk) matching your working paper files can be created and called, for instance, Work WP (for word processing files). Within the subdirectory for, say Marketing, you can have a file called Pricing, one called Promotion, and one called Ideas. A Personnel subdirectory can be established and within it you can have a file for each of your personnel and all correspondence to them can be recorded there. Figure 2.8 illustrates organization of word processing files.

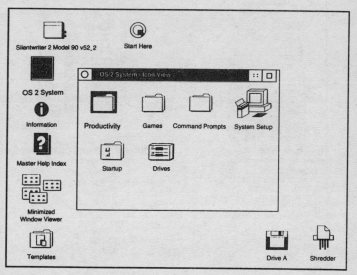

Figure 2.7. Computer Windows screen.

WORD PROCESSING FILES

Many users save large numbers of files. This is okay provided that you can easily retrieve files you need. Word processing packages often do not permit lengthy filenames, making identification of contents difficult. The key is to create directories that effectively segment your files into similar groups:

Difficult to Retrieve	Easy to Retrieve	
GCIRAUSS.LT	Directory -	GOVTCONT
GCIRAUSC.PR	Subdirectory -	IRS
GCIRFIMN.PR	Subdirectory -	AUDITS
GCIRFIWJ.LT		SAMSMITH.LT
		SUECOOK.PRO
	Subdirectory -	FINES
		MARYNASH.PRO
		WMJAMES.LT

ELECTRONIC AND PAPER FILES SYSTEMS PARALLEL AND REINFORCE EACH OTHER

PAPER WORKING FILES

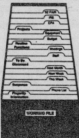

PAPER REFERENCE FILES

E-MAIL FOLDERS
(working and short-term reference)

- ADMIN
- FINGERTIP REFERENCE
- GOVT CONTRACTS
- MAIN
- MEETINGS
- NONGOVT CONTRACTS
- PEOPLE
- PENDING
- SUSPENSE
- TRADE FAIRS

WORD PROCESSING DIRECTORIES
(reference)

ADMIN
    BUDGET
    PERSONNEL
    EQUIPMENT
GOVTCONT
    EPA
    IRS
NONGOVT
TRADFAIR

Figure 2.8. Word processing files.

An electronic equivalent for a paper Reference file for forms might be a directory called Forms and within it subdirectories called Sample Letters, and Offers, can be stored and easily retrieved.

The same procedure can be applied to any spreadsheet application you may have. The directory might be called Worksprd. Sht. A Budget subdirectory can be created and within it you may have a file for a Cost spreadsheet. Another file might contain a Cash Flow spreadsheet. You might create a subdirectory for Results and include files with a spreadsheet for each Region or Office and a file possibly named Combined providing you with combined results of these different files.

HANDLING AND ORGANIZING E-MAIL

It is much faster and easier to retrieve documents in the computer when the computer is organized along the lines of directories, subdirectories, and files.

Some people routinely receive 150 to 200 E-mail, or electronic mail, messages a day, which can be overwhelming. To keep this load manageable you'll need to apply most of the principles related to paper-based files. Systems vary widely, but certain basic habits should be established to make the system work for you.

Like your in basket, your electronic mailbox can fill up quickly. Some systems allow hundreds of messages to accumulate. This can become unmanageable and cause slowdowns. An overworked and overloaded computer is slow to retrieve messages—not to mention the person who has to read it all! Accordingly, the rule for electronic mail is this: *DO IT NOW; DELETE IT NOW.*

Act on and respond to your messages the first time you read them. Don't let your electronic mailbox become cluttered with messages you've read—use your delete key often! Messages that you do keep should be stored in the correct computer directory or electronic "folder," or if printed out, in the correct working file.

Many E-mail applications allow you to create storage "folders" for those messages you wish to keep but do not want to leave in the same location as your incoming E-mail. You can name one of these folders Pending for those messages for which you are awaiting input or a response. You might have a folder called Procedures for those E-mail messages establishing procedures or policy.

In summary, you'll want to set up electronic directories that parallel your working files and your reference files. Move items you need to save on a short-term basis to the correct directory immediately. For longer-term reference and archive documents, use whatever storage medium is available to you that will permit the easiest retrieval, whether by storing on floppy disk or by printing out. Figure 2.9 shows how to organize E-mail files.

Beware of printouts, however, unless they're absolutely necessary! There is no need to add to your own paper crunch, and it is irresponsible and unnecessary to print out one or two lines on an otherwise blank sheet of paper. If the message pertains to an ongoing project you already have a paper file on, write the few pertinent sentences down on an existing sheet of paper in your files in the form of an update. Better yet, start keeping your updates in electronic form using software designed for this purpose.

The handling of voice mail follows some of the same principles, except there is no easy way to "file" the information. When dealing with voice mail messages, *Do It Now*! Take each message as far as you can, and when you leave voice mail messages, leave complete messages. Write messages down, either in a logbook or in the appropriate working file. If you need to follow up on the subject in the future, write messages down in your calendar.

Both E-mail and voice mail are excellent production tools. They are fast and easy to use. But you need to seriously organize these tools or they can overwhelm you.

ORGANIZING OTHER MEDIA

Other items such as books, shelves, briefcase, Rolodex, and business cards also need to be well organized. Figure 2.10 provides some guidance.

ORGANIZING E-MAIL FILES

Most E-mail systems allow you to set up "folders" to store messages in. You should follow principles similar to those used in organizing your paper files:

❑ Separate action items from reference items.
❑ Establish folders for each key function or project for which you have responsibility.
❑ Establish a suspense (tickler) system. Sometimes this is best done in conjunction with other software, such as calendaring or personal information management software.
❑ Group similar functions so it is easy to locate the appropriate folder.

Here's how your folders could be set up:

E - MAIL FOLDERS

Admin Budget
Admin Equipment
Admin Personnel

Fingertip Reference

Govt Contract - EPA
Govt Contract - IRS

Main

Meetings - Quality Task Force
Meetings - Weekly Staff

NONGOVT CONTRACTS

People
Pending
Personal

Suspense - This Week
Suspense - Next Week
Suspense - Next Month

Trade Fairs - Regional
Trade Fairs - National

The working folders that contain files that still need to be acted on would be:

Main folder: Items you'll respond to today

Meetings: Items for group discussion or follow through.

People folder: Copies of items you've delegated, for purposes of follow-up.

Pending: Copies of messages sent for which you are awaiting a response.

Suspense: Items you are scheduling to address later.

The rest of the folders are **SHORT-TERM REFERENCE** and will need to be deleted, transferred, or archived periodically.

Figure 2.9. E-mail files organization.

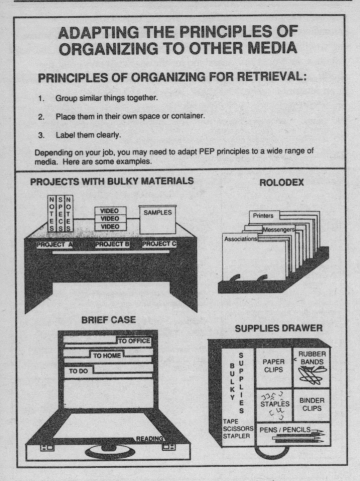

ADAPTING THE PRINCIPLES OF ORGANIZING TO OTHER MEDIA

PRINCIPLES OF ORGANIZING FOR RETRIEVAL:

1. Group similar things together.

2. Place them in their own space or container.

3. Label them clearly.

Depending on your job, you may need to adapt PEP principles to a wide range of media. Here are some examples.

PROJECTS WITH BULKY MATERIALS

NOTES SPECS NOTES
VIDEO VIDEO VIDEO SAMPLES
PROJECT A PROJECT B PROJECT C

ROLODEX

Printers
Messengers
Associations

BRIEF CASE

TO OFFICE
TO HOME
TO DO
READING

SUPPLIES DRAWER

BULKY SUPPLIES | PAPER CLIPS | RUBBER BANDS
| STAPLES | BINDER CLIPS
TAPE SCISSORS STAPLER | PENS / PENCILS

Figure 2.10. Organizing other media.

It isn't easy to get organized. At first the task may seem overwhelming. I'm reminded of the scene in the movie *Jaws*, where the sheriff, the eccentric shark hunter, and the scientist are on the boat together, far out at sea, searching for the shark. At one point the sheriff goes out on deck to toss scraps of meat and blood overboard in an attempt to attract the shark. Well, his luck couldn't be better. The shark rises up out of the water, dwarfing the sheriff, the boat, and everything within sight. The terrified sheriff plasters himself against the boathouse and mutters, "We're going to need a bigger boat."

And sometimes that's how reorganization feels. However, if you'll press on, you will survive the ordeal. Nothing in the world can take the place of persistence, and it will be well worth your efforts.

FOLLOW-UP FOR CHAPTER 2

1. Clear the backlog and organize your work area. Very likely you will require a day or more to do this. If at all possible, schedule this time so you work undisturbed.

2. Get at least three trays and mark them "In," "Pending," and "Out." Your in basket will receive all new material. Your pending basket is for those things you cannot do now, for things that are out of your control. Your out basket is for all those papers you've completed.

3. Empty out onto your desk every piece of paper or document from your drawers, trays, walls, and briefcase. Look everywhere— under the blotter, behind the curtain, under the desk.

4. Pick up the top piece of paper and deal with it *now*! You should:
   (a) Deal with it until completed.
   (b) Deal with it as completely as you can and then place it in the pending basket if very short term or the tickler file under the appropriate date while awaiting a response.

(c) Delegate it.

(d) Create a pile on the floor for papers needed for ongoing work or projects to file in your working files.

(e) Create another pile on the floor for papers to file in the reference file, if it's information you need but which requires you to do nothing at the moment.

(f) Create a pile on the floor for papers to file in the archive file.

(g) Throw it away! Do this if it's trivial, of no use, already dealt with, or exists elsewhere.

5. Treat backlogs on your computer (E-mail, for example) in the same way.

6. After all this, set up your working files. Create hang files and labels for each work project and general category. Create files and labels for the reference files and archive files.

7. Create individual follow-up files for each of your subordinates and your boss or peers with whom you have regular contact. Label each file with the person's name, and place in that file notes about things you need to check on regarding ongoing, long-term projects.

8. Create a tickler file. The tickler file is part of your working files. If you have a secretary, the tickler file should be maintained at the secretary's desk.

9. Take time to understand your computer's operating system facilities to organize your computer files. Hard disk (general categories such as databases and spreadsheet), desktop (objects or icons grouped similarly to your hard disk categories), files within your individual applications should be organized into directories and subdirectories, and so forth. Organize your computer information to match your paper organization as closely as your computer's software allows.

10. Avoid confusion in setting up your word processing files by taking time to organize your electronic storage space into directories and subdirectories that effectively segment your files into similar groups, using names that fit your computer system's limitations.

11. Make a list of missing supplies and tools necessary for you to do your job: tape, staples, extra file folders, labels, pens, formatted disks, scissors, envelopes, stamps, and anything else you may need. Make sure you have them all on hand and that everything works.

12. Now, make a list of all the things you've had bouncing around inside your brain to do: the small bits and pieces of bad conscience, the not-so-urgent items, the little things you may have been putting off. Dump it all out of your head and onto paper. Once you've listed everything, start acting on each item, beginning from the top of the list. Don't stop until you've worked your way through every item on your list. That's how you'll know when you're done.

That's it. Get going. *Do It Now!*

CHAPTER 3
Do It Routinely

We are what we repeatedly do.
—ARISTOTLE

Chapter 3 Preview

In this chapter, you will learn how to:

- Organize your schedule and work to operate within large blocks of time.
- Batch your work. Schedule time to process mail and memos all at once. Handle telephone calls, E-mail, and so forth, the same way.
- Eliminate low-value information and prevent it from coming to you in the first place.
- Stamp out time-consuming and unnecessary interruptions.
- Hold scheduled one-on-one meetings weekly with your direct reports to improve communication and process work efficiently.

You will increase your efficiency and effectiveness (your productivity) by working smarter on the right things. The simple key to personal productivity is to batch many job-related activities and do them routinely. The idea is to spend a minimum amount of time on the relatively unimportant things so that you can spend a maximum amount of time on important things.

Of course, first you must determine the important things—what you should be working on first—and then discover ways to do the work you identify as important more efficiently and effectively.

First you should assess how you currently spend your time. Next ask yourself, "Would the results be better if I spent my time working on some other activity?" Then ask yourself, "How could I do the high-level activities more frequently and efficiently?"

KEEP A TIME LOG

To identify precisely how you spend your time, keep a time log. In his landmark book *The Effective Executive* (Harper & Row, 1966), Peter Drucker says that we can't hope to control our time until we know where our time goes. No doubt we think we know where our time goes, but most of us don't. Drucker (p. 27) writes:

> I sometimes ask executives who pride themselves on their memory to put down their guess as to how they spend their own time. Then I lock these guesses away for a few weeks or months. In the meantime, the executives run an actual time record on themselves. There is never much resemblance between the way these men thought they used their time and their actual records

Only by keeping a time log will you get an accurate idea of where your time is being spent. I have often used this technique with clients who are especially busy. Their workload is so great that they do not have a clear picture of the nature of their workload to be able to address it effectively. Keeping a record not only tells them what they spend their time on, it also gives insight into who might be dropping the ball in their area, what functions might not be covered, and how they might be wasting the time of others.

To avoid making this time log an administrative burden, simply keep a piece of paper on your desk. As you deal with things, you note what it was, how long it took, and who was involved. Figure 3.1 is a sample form of a time log. Soon categories of things begin to become visible.

After a couple of weeks of keeping records, tally it all up. You will have a pretty good idea where your time goes. You can then start addressing the areas of waste and inefficiency.

OVERCOME INFORMATION OVERLOAD

We all experience a flood of information. It can be overwhelming, and it can blind us to what we should be focused on. In this information age, we need to know what information we *don't* need as much as we need to know what information we do need.

The best way to overcome information overload is to stop low-value information and tasks from entering your system. Figure 3.2 shows the different ways to screen information. Back-end screening, meaning allowing all information to arrive unfiltered and sorting through it after the fact, is the least effective way of controlling the flow of information to you. A better method of information control would be to have the information screened before it gets to you. Having this done by support staff is better yet. The ideal solution is to carefully analyze all sources of information and eliminate at the source the nonessential information by removing yourself from the distribution list, canceling the subscription, and so forth.

BEYOND THE IN BASKET

Paper in your in basket, voice mail and E-mail messages, telephone calls, and people all clamor for your attention. Add to this all the

	Activity	Person	Subject
7:00			
:15			
:30			
:45			
8:00			
:15			
:30			
:45			
9:00			
:15			
:30			
:45			
10:00			
:15			
:30			
:45			
11:00			
:15			
:30			
:45			
12:00			
:15			
:30			
:45			
1:00			
:15			
:30			
:45			
2:00			
:15			
:30			
:45			
3:00			
:15			
:30			
:45			
4:00			
:15			
:30			
:45			
5:00			
:15			
:30			
:45			
6:00			
:15			
:30			
:45			

Figure 3.1. Sample time log form.

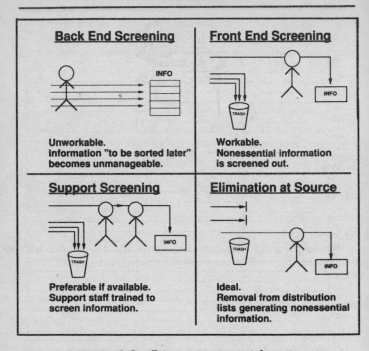

Figure 3.2. Four ways to screen information.

meetings you must attend, and it's no wonder you feel you rarely accomplish anything important.

I've watched people whose idea of a productive day at work is to spend the entire day at their desk going through the items that come into their in basket. They are fully occupied doing just those things.

Too much of what comes into your in basket daily is the after-the-fact proof of someone else's accomplishment. It's done, over with, and probably 50 percent of it is for your information and files. Rarely, if ever, does it make the company money. So often what you process is

relatively unimportant. That's why I recommend you dedicate minimum time to it and get on with your real work.

The way to control this often overwhelming flow of information is to categorize and group it and organize an efficient response to it.

BATCH THE ROUTINE WORK

The categorizing and grouping of your work might be called "batching." Each piece of paper, each E-mail message, every telephone call, every interruption, and every item you send out is a form of communication. Process similar communications and tasks in batches, reducing waste and motion. You'll complete each task more efficiently.

Many elements of your work can be reduced to simple routines that will let you complete similar tasks in the shortest possible time. These tasks readily lend themselves to batching. The advantages of approaching your work in this way are numerous.

It is easier to take a batch of completed work from your out basket and distribute it all at the same time, than getting up from your desk each time one piece of work is completed.

73

It saves time to do all word processing work at once instead of going in and out of the different applications each time you have new word processing to do.

There is less effort involved in doing all filing at once than filing each paper individually.

You will find batching like work allows you to prepare and organize yourself for the work one time instead of many times if the work is done randomly.

SCHEDULE AND AVOID HAVING TO DECIDE

It's important to juggle between acting on everything as it comes up and always putting things off to do later. There is a way to deal with this. I refer to it as *Do It Now, Later.* Schedule times to do certain work (such as opening and reading your mail) and when the time arrives, *Do It Now.* Don't look at it until you are prepared to act. When you do look at it, act on it. *Do It Now, Later.*

If you want to get something done, schedule it. Since these in-basket tasks rarely represent the most important part of your job, they are seldom considered priority, so they don't get done. The hidden consequence of this clutter and information overload is to slow down the whole process of your important work. If you have to choose between calling the customer or sorting through your in basket, what are you going to do? If you're like most people, you'll choose the customer, right? But the other things don't get done! What you want to do is avoid putting yourself in the position of having to constantly decide between things. It makes your life harder than it has to be. Instead, schedule a time to go through your in basket and do other routine tasks that can be batched. When the time arrives to do that particular task, do it during the time allotted and move on to the work that is important.

Do you brush your teeth in the morning? "Yes," you say. Do you think about brushing your teeth? Do you prioritize it? Do you wonder "Am I going to brush my teeth now, or am I going to have a cup of coffee?'' Probably not. It's part of a nonthinking routine you've established as part of your habits. You don't burden yourself with lots of thought about it. In fact you hardly give it any thought. Through force of habit, you eliminated the steps of conscious decision making. You simply do it routinely. And that's the way you want to handle these simple batched tasks.

PARKINSON'S LAW AND THE ALLOCATION OF TIME

Parkinson's law says *work tends to fill up (adjust to) the time available or allotted for it.* If you only allocate one hour to complete a certain task you have a much greater chance of finishing the work in that time. If you set a deadline to complete a project by a certain date you will likely figure out how to do it within the time you set for that deadline.

BLOCKS OF TIME

Working in blocks of time is more efficient and effective than working piecemeal. This not only applies to the batching of similar tasks, such as telephone calls, or to the handling of incoming mail, but also to project work, sales calls, or to a marketing campaign. Peter Drucker suggests that the ideal span of time to work is ninety minutes. You will get more done in a concentrated period of ninety minutes than twice the time in an environment of regular interruptions. Blocking out undisturbed time will greatly increase your productivity. If you manage to get the many little tasks out of the way first, you will be better able to focus during your uninterrupted blocks of time. You'll feel good knowing you've covered all the important issues and organized your time and your work to permit you to do the important things. Giving your mind enough time to get into the heart of the issue is far more productive than being constantly distracted from the work at hand by other tasks that crop up, demanding your attention.

Some of us may not have an office door to close, and so we have to be more creative if we are to enjoy blocks of undisturbed time. One client's company was composed of account officers who worked together in a noisy, open-office environment where the phone rang continuously as clients initiated transactions. In part of the building were several small interview offices. When an account officer needed a block of time to put together a proposal, another officer would cover for her as she used the interview room to peacefully complete the proposal.

Another client would work out of a home office one day per week. This particular client found that working at home afforded him the time he needed for strategic planning and prospecting for new business.

BATCHING TELEPHONE CALLS

Decide that you will not accept calls haphazardly throughout the work day; instead, you will return calls (depending on the nature of your job) perhaps once or twice during the day. If you accept calls twice a day, say between 11:30 A.M. and 12:00 P.M. and between 4:00 P.M. and 5:00 P.M., simply tell your assistant you will not accept calls at other times. This doesn't mean you want your assistant to "hold" your calls—it means that you establish a routine: you take phone calls at certain times, except in specific cases. Of course, you then have to define those specific cases. You will probably accept calls from an important client or your immediate supervisor, for example, and you will want to establish clear parameters for "emergency" calls.

Be sure all of the office staff clearly understands the new procedure, who and what the exceptions would be, and how messages are to be taken. To return a call you have to understand the message.

"Bill called" is not acceptable by itself. Ask assistants to take *complete, correct* messages. Train your assistants how to find out what Bill wants and when Bill will be available to discuss the subject: "Bill called to schedule an appointment with the sales team in New York. He will be available all afternoon at such-and-such number." This allows you to prepare yourself for the call. You know what the call is all about, and you know when you can reach him. When you reach Bill, you can have your calendar open and suggest several times and alternative days when you're available to meet. You'll impress Bill and wrap up the call in minimal time.

If you have voice mail or an answering service, you could create a message that conveys the same information:

> *"Hello, this is Frank. I'm not available to take your call at the moment. If you would leave a complete message, I will prepare for our conversation and get back to you as soon as I can. I normally return phone calls between 11:00 A.M. and noon, eastern time. Please let me know if that's a convenient time for you. If it isn't, please suggest another time you might be available."*

Now, you have to stick to the new procedure. Stick to the routine of returning all phone calls at a given time in the day, and stick to your procedure of refusing calls at any other time (within the guidelines you establish).

In this way, you'll be prepared to return your calls, and you can organize yourself for them. You can consult files or documents before returning the call. You can have all pertinent material in front of you so you don't waste time. Treat your calls precisely as you treat the items in your in basket—one at a time, working through them to completion. In scheduling these call times allow sufficient flexibility to handle calls that depend on varying time zones, emergencies, and other special circumstances.

E-MAIL

Some people routinely receive hundreds of E-mail messages a day, which can be overwhelming, but you can manage this load if you establish good habits and make the system work for you.

When sending E-mail:

- Discuss one subject per message.
- Clearly define the topic in the message header.
- Keep your message brief but include all information necessary for the recipient to act or correspond.
- Don't overdistribute mail.

Processing E-mail normally needs to be done more often than once a day. E-mail has become a substitute for the telephone and needs to be acted on. How do you handle this? I suggest that you handle your E-mail three or four times a day. Nobody expects a response in two hours. If they do, they would likely call on the telephone. When you do look at E-mail, process all of it. Handle it, file it, purge it, do it. The rule for electronic mail is this: *Do It Now, Delete It Now!*

If you have a beeper alert function in your E-mail system, your system will beep every time a message comes in. I highly recommend you turn it off. You do not need to be distracted every five minutes with something you are not going to do.

When it is time to respond to your messages, act on them as you first read them. Don't let your E-mail box become cluttered with messages you've read—use your delete key often! Store messages that you keep in the correct E-mail folder or, if printed out, in the right working file.

MAIL/MEMOS

Deal with your mail and internal office memos once a day at a set time, perhaps first thing in the morning before the normal meetings and activities begin. Depending on the nature of your work, allow thirty to sixty minutes to process all of the paper that accumulates in your in box during the day. If you have an administrative assistant, have him or her hold all incoming paperwork after you complete your pass at the in box. Ask your assistant to sort the incoming material into logical categories and to use a divider system to organize incoming material and make it easy for you to process. After purging the inevitable junk mail, have your assistant put the incoming papers into your in basket at the end of the day and place items for other people to deal with in their boxes. Then you don't have to go through other people's materials. Included in your incoming papers would be any papers from your tickler file that are scheduled for your attention that day.

Some managers invite their administrative assistants to sit in with them while they deal with their in basket. In this case, the assistant files as they go along, notes instructions, and generally helps the manager process the work quickly. This, by the way, is how I advise managers to train new administrative assistants. The manager should process the paperwork out loud, so the assistant gets a sense for how the manager deals with things, what is important to the manager, and what the manager wants to see and not see. I find a couple of weeks of this equals a year's worth of experience working together.

Whether you work with an assistant or not, don't just sort through your papers. Do each item, one by one, responding, routing, reading, and filing as you go along. If a paper is part of a working project you will be acting on at a scheduled time in the future, file it immediately in your working file. If a paper prompts an origination from you, originate it now. If it's something you need to discuss with a subordinate or your boss and it's not a burning issue, file it in your working file under his or her name for discussion at your scheduled meeting time. If it's something to read, read it.

Make no exceptions to the rule. This is a moment of truth. If a paper represents two or three hours work, schedule a time to deal with it, and file the paper into the scheduled date in your tickler file. But mainly *Do It Now* and empty your in box of all papers that were there. Some won't be all that important, but deal with them anyway.

Some might say looking at your papers once a day is not enough. Well, I disagree and so do 150,000 clients. Very important issues normally find their way to you in the form of telephone calls, personal visits, or E-mail. Since most people do not deal with their paper promptly, they don't depend on it for hot issues that need to be dealt with in a matter of minutes. If you *did* process your paper completely every day you would surprise your coworkers at your promptness!

READING

Your reading should be handled in the same way. Set aside a block of time and do it however works best for you. Some of your reading will be done when you process your mail and memos. Remember when you pick up a piece of paper, you are going to deal with it then and there. Some people do their reading during the morning commute by bus or train; some during plane flights; others take a few minutes at the end of the work day to do their reading and organize for the coming work day. I do my reading during my lunch break. The important thing is to find a time to do it and establish it as a routine. Assign yourself a time, schedule it, and do it.

When you read is one issue; *how* you read is another. Speed reading can cut your reading time in half by training you to look at the material from a concept, sentence, paragraph, or page perspective, instead of word by word, which is how most of us have been taught to read. There is no loss of content comprehension. You simply comprehend more, faster!

WEEKLY ONE-ON-ONE MEETINGS

Another item that comes under the heading of "routine" are the weekly one-on-one meetings between the boss and his or her direct reports.

One-on-one meetings make for efficient contact time between busy coworkers who have to maintain close contacts in their work.

If the only way colleagues can see you is by sticking their head in during the day at random, you will be constantly interrupted. They will feel guilty about disturbing you, but they know they must if they are going to get the job done. You won't be prepared for discussion on the subject they disturb you about. Or vice versa if you are the one interrupting.

You may argue that you can't handle another meeting. However, many managers are managers in name only. With downsizing, companies are forcing managers to have many more duties than simply managing. You need an efficient way to keep in touch with those who answer to you and who get the work done.

This is not a team or group meeting. It's one-on-one. Maintain a file for every person you meet with one-on-one, and during the course of the week, collect any nonpriority items you need to discuss. Also, each person who reports to you should maintain a similar folder, covering items they need to talk about with you.

Schedule one-on-one meetings for the same time every week. If it isn't scheduled, people can't depend on it, and they will revert to coming to see you at any odd time. If you travel often or a holiday period makes it difficult to keep to the same schedule, make it a point at the end of your one-to-one to schedule the next one-to-one meeting, taking the holiday into account.

Remember, these meetings cover nonpriority items that crop up and can wait a few days to be resolved or answered, not things that demand an immediate solution.

DEALING WITH INTERRUPTIONS

Not all interruptions are bad, of course. There are actually some good interruptions. If your associate pokes his head in your doorway and says, "Hey, listen, I had this bright idea about how to get a sale, and I'd like to make a call," that's what I'd call a good interruption.

Still there are more ways to cut down on unwanted interruptions. Here are some tried-and-true ways which should sound familiar to you:

Do It Now!

- Clean up backlogs so you're not dealing with their consequences.
- Handle things by due date to reduce requests for status reports.

Do It "Right" Now

- Handle things completely and correctly to reduce redo requests.
- Give clear and complete instructions to subordinates to reduce their requests for clarification and your own frustrations when things are not done correctly the first time.
- Remember that it is your job to educate your employees in how to complete both routine tasks and larger jobs.

Communicate It "Right" Now

- Give full information when leaving messages to reduce phone tag.
- Require complete messages be taken when others call you.
- Use communication methods that permit full messages and do not interrupt current work, such as E-mail and voice mail.

"Take a Stand" Now

- Deal with interruptions by stating your time constraints: "Jim, I have twenty minutes to complete this report for a meeting. Let

me stop by your office after that meeting and we'll discuss this. Is 2:30 all right with you?"
- Reinforce this by standing up to deal with walk-in interruptions.
- Lend support to creating a culture with fewer interruptions.
- Begin batching your communications.

By batching work you can cut down on interruptions (see Figure 3.3), allowing you to better focus on the work on hand.

MAKING IT WORK

You may think: "Hey I don't want to schedule my life down to the minute" or "This represents an ideal world and my office is far from ideal." These scheduled activities should require no more than 20 percent of your day. Since all my research shows that you are spending well over *half* of your day on these things now you can thank me for giving you back at least 25 percent of your day.

I don't like having my day scheduled to the minute either. But most of what I'm asking you to do here is to handle the mindless and boring tasks efficiently and routinely. We have to do the mundane if we're to concentrate on what we are truly being paid for. So, why not just face up to it and do it? Get it over with in as painless a fashion as possible. Then the remainder of your day can be made up of blocks of time to concentrate and focus on the meaningful activities of your work.

PITFALLS

One problem people sometimes face early on in learning to work this way is that they sometimes choose the wrong time to do certain things. You may decide to return all your phone calls at 4:00 P.M. every day, regardless of circumstances, when in fact, because you're on the West Coast, it's impossible for you to reach anyone east of

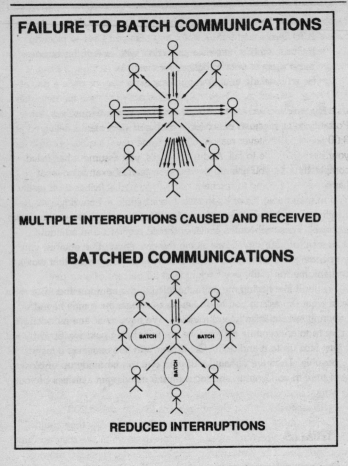

Figure 3.3. Batching communications reduces interruptions.

Denver at that time. The logical thing to do is to allow a few moments between 8:00 A.M. and 9:00 A.M. for any calls you have to place to the East Coast; there's no reason you can't take care of this business before moving on to your in basket, for example.

Or you may decide to answer your mail and memos once a day at 10:00 A.M. without fail. Of course, that's exactly the time the new staff meeting is scheduled or, for reasons known only to themselves, the Postal Service readjusts its schedule and your daily mail is delivered at 3:00 P.M. For whatever reason, after just one day it's quite possible for your new schedule to fail. And since it fails, you assume it has failed completely, and you give up the effort, instead of examining what happened and trying to reschedule your planned activities to fit reality. You may discover it's more feasible to draft memos between 11:45 A.M. and 12:15 P.M., or even 12:00 P.M. to 12:30 P.M. since you seldom get out the door to lunch until then anyway, and schedule 3:30 P.M. to 4:00 P.M. to respond to the day's mail. The point is, you may have to try several times before you find the schedule that works best for you.

Trial and error is often required in getting the job done and in learning new ways to get jobs done. For example, you may have to have people cover for you while you do some of the batched work we talked about. If you have a customer service job, for example, you may not be able to turn off your phone. Or your work may depend on walk-in customers, and you may never know when a customer is going to arrive. Certainly, when customers do walk in, you want to see them and answer their needs.

I had a client who had five employees to deal with 3,000 customers, mostly by telephone and fax. But every day they could expect ten or so unannounced customers to arrive to see their account representative. The visits were mainly social and considered more or less a waste of time. But they were customers, and the employees wanted to treat them well. This created a real problem. They wanted to give good service, but the unannounced arrivals created havoc on their schedules and work. This problem existed for years and nothing seemed to make it go away. They finally organized the department so each account rep was on duty to see all unannounced customer visits one day per week, leaving four days per week where each rep was able to get on with his or her work. I can't tell you how many other solutions they tried, though, before they tried this rather simple one and found that it worked.

As you attempt to put some of these principles into practice, you'll find some trial and error is required, too. Persistence counts. If you work on the problem, you'll not only come up with a solution, but with a solution that works for you.

We all know how difficult it is to overcome habits and years of conditioning. Habitual behaviors usually don't change on the first attempt. Your first fourteen tries may appear to be failures. But then something clicks on the fifteenth try, and you find everything falling into place. Even when you do finally get into the new habit, it isn't necessarily easier to do unpleasant or boring tasks. Every time I wake at 5:30 A.M. to go running, I find it is tough. But, scheduling the routine behavior helps me to do it. If the running were not a habit, I would surely find it even tougher and I would likely not do it at all.

Let scheduling and simple habits make life easier for you.

FOLLOW-UP FOR CHAPTER 3

1. Work smarter. You can increase your efficiency and effectiveness (productivity) by working smarter. Only you can determine what requires and deserves your attention. Regardless of what those things are, you can make more time for them by working smart on everything. Simple routines to handle the mundane tasks can help you do exactly that.

2. Analyze your time. If you've never analyzed how and where you spend your time, this can be very useful. Use a time log to keep track of what you do and how long it takes. You'll be amazed at how much time you spend on certain items and how little time you spend on others. Once you know what you're doing, you can work on how you do it.

3. Don't allow low-value tasks or low-value information to enter your system. Both clog your ability to produce. Screen them out entirely. Delegate tasks appropriately. Direct information you don't use to someone else's attention. Dedicate minimal time to routine work, such as the incoming mail. Take care of it promptly and routinely, and move on to high-value work.

4. Learn how to batch work. Return phone calls once or twice daily, rather than allowing them to constantly interrupt your work. Do the same with your incoming mail. Set aside a time each day to work through each item to completion, or schedule items to work on at appropriate times in the short-term future. If you batch work instead of letting unimportant tasks dominate your day, you'll find you have about 25 percent more time to dedicate to important work. Answering phone messages, responding to memos, handling your E-mail are all tasks you should handle by batching.

5. *Do It Now, Later* means sticking to a schedule. If you're in the middle of a report when your mail is delivered, continue to work on the report. Schedule thirty minutes daily to handle your mail and do it then. Don't break off in the middle of one task to take on another. If you do, both are likely to end up unfinished as the second task is interrupted by a third task.

6. Schedule tasks (and you have less to worry about). If scheduled, you simply do them and move on. If you allot an hour for a particular task, you will likely complete it within an hour. If you allot a day for the same task, you will likely take all day to complete it.

7. Schedule weekly one-on-one meetings for routine items concerning your direct reports. This will eliminate most interruptions and will allow you regular time periods to touch base with one another regarding ongoing projects and personal items. You should maintain a file for each of your people and make a habit of dropping reminders into it to prompt your meeting agendas. Your direct reports should keep a similar file for you, to prompt their discussion during these meetings. Remember, these meetings are for nonpriority items that can wait a week to be resolved and not for emergencies.

8. Review the steps you can use to eliminate interruptions and then put them into practice.

Plan It Now

*All difficult things have their origin in that which is easy,
and great things in that which is small.*
—LAO-TZU

Chapter 4 Preview

In this chapter, you will learn:

- Time flies by when you are in a state of preoccupation. Thinking about what you are supposed to do instead of planning efficiently is a major cause of wasted time.
- Action follows clarity of picture. If you have a clear picture of what you are to do, you will act on it. If the picture is fuzzy, you will hesitate. Planning gives clarity of picture.
- To establish what is important to you.
- To write down your goals (those that will define what you value).
- To establish an efficient planning process by setting aside time each week to organize yourself, review your goals and plans, and plan out the new week.

This may surprise you, but the motto for the planning step of the personal efficiency program (PEP) is *Plan It Now!*

One purpose of planning is to *get clarity*, to know what you ought to be doing on a day-to-day basis as well as on a long-term basis. Too many people do very little planning, particularly when their own work is involved. One reason why the personal calendar, planner, or organizer (Day-Timer, Franklin Planner, and others) made such a hit when it appeared on the market in the 1980s is that people saw it as an opportunity or a tool to help them get organized, to plan things in advance, and to keep track of work done.

Some mistakenly consider the mental activities they engage in when they're driving to work or when they're taking a shower to be "planning" for work. Although you may be thinking about work, I would hardly call it planning. Instead, it's an inefficient form of thinking that provides little or no real clarity.

Some people feel that any and all planning is a waste of time. They say the time spent in planning doesn't produce that many benefits. If you plan inefficiently, that can be true. If what you plan is not what you do, it is wasteful. A set plan is only good if it is being implemented and accomplished. If what you do is what you plan, then planning is meaningful.

If you feel that you're under stress at work; that you have too much to do, and too little time to do it; that you're out of control; or that you're simply not accomplishing the things most important to you, you may find that the cause is often poor planning or the lack of planning. In that case, you'll find the products you produce bear a resemblance to the bumper sticker, "plan ahead," where the word "ahead" is all crunched up on the right side.

That's typical, primarily because people don't connect planning to what they do personally. They think of planning in terms of the huge project their department is undertaking during this fiscal quarter—a project so huge that they'll all get together for a meeting and figure out what to do. But when it comes to their daily work, they don't put a proper importance to planning.

PURPOSE OF PLANNING

The purpose of the planning process is to get a clear idea—a clear mental picture—of what you need to do. A planning process can only be considered effective if it provides you with a clear picture, because you can't act without a picture. In his book *The Management of Time* (Prentice-Hall, Inc., 1959), James T. McCay writes:

> *The pictures in your mind control your actions. If you have no picture; if, you can't make out what is going on, you don't act. If your pictures are cloudy and confused, you act hesitantly. If your pictures are clear and accurate, you act definitely and effectively.*

Planning enables you to get these clear pictures. Planning that fails to provide such images falls short of the mark and isn't true planning.

When doing PEP with a large group, we start out with an orientation, usually in a conference room with everyone seated around a table. I often ask: "How many people in here do a daily action plan?" Perhaps half the people raise their hands. The rest don't even commit themselves to daily action plans. Too often these daily To Do lists have failed for them in the past, and they're reluctant to try them again.

Have you ever started the day with a list of things to do and come to the end of the day with none of the tasks done? If so, you know how many of these people feel. Daily action plans can weigh one down: They're the evidence of unfinished business. There are several reasons for unfinished lists. You might have tried to do too much. You may not have considered the unexpected and the time consumed. The daily list may have been far too general. Proper planning successfully deals with these and many other issues that make a daily plan a disappointment rather than a useful work tool. What is proper planning?

To give an example, let's look at what it takes to make a movie. Three distinct steps are involved in the production of a movie: preproduction, production, and postproduction. Of the three, the most time-consuming element of making the movie is preproduction. The script is only the starting point. The most essential planning document in the preproduction phase is known as the "story board," a detailed, artistic representation of every single scene that will make up the movie.

Picture a sheet of paper filled only with empty boxes; sometimes, you'll even find them in the familiar shape of a television screen. These boxes make up the frames for each scene. Artists sketch in rough outlines to represent what is seen at every point of filming: how many people and who are in a particular scene; what they say; whether a scene is shot in close up or with a long lens; where the lights are; the step by step progression from one shot to the next, the combination of shots adding up to a single scene, all part of the much larger whole—a motion picture.

Why spend so much time and effort on a story board? Because one of the most expensive parts of movie making is the on-location shooting. Once production is underway, with two hundred cast members standing around, you want to waste little time and effort, not to mention money, telling people where they stand and what they do next. That's what preproduction is for, not production. With millions of dollars invested, you simply don't waste time when adequate planning and preparation will save you that time and effort.

In the motion picture industry, the need for planning is obvious and the technique of planning has been refined to meet that industry's particular needs. Yet in business and industry in general, there is little formal planning, especially the planning of day-to-day activities.

Take a mental step back from your own company, and you'll see that most of the people you work with everyday don't have any formal planning in their work. We see people showing up for work without any script or preproduction planning, merely hoping to handle the fallout for eight or more hours. In motion picture terms they're on the set every day of the work week, the cameras are rolling, and they don't know what to say, where to stand, or what to do.

PEP PLANNING PROCESS

Six general categories of planning are taught in PEP:

1. Daily plan.
2. Weekly plan.
3. Project implementation plan.
4. Strategic plan.
5. Goal setting.
6. Values.

DAILY PLANNING

I've already mentioned a common complaint about daily plans. Too often, due to the unexpected, the daily plan is only partially done before it turns into a major disappointment. For some people, it seems, daily plans are only a mocking reminder of what didn't get done.

In the meantime, it's vital that you understand the importance of spending some time each day to plan your activities. Some prefer to do this at the end of the day, before going home; some prefer the morning, before other things get in the way. Whenever you choose to do this planning, you can use your calendar ("diary," as the British say) to write down the day's tasks.

To make daily planning an efficient and quick process, I suggest you create your daily plan from a weekly plan. With the larger document in front of you, you can then divide the week's work into manageable chunks to be accomplished each day, knowing every day that you're working toward a larger goal.

WEEKLY PLANNING

Once a week you should examine all of your sources of work as shown in Figure 4.1. By "sources of work" I mean all of your working files, including your projects, your calendar for deadlines, scheduled activities and reminders, your tickler file system for the things that will be showing up during the upcoming week, your pending matters (pending basket, pending files), any logbook you may keep to record the things you must do.

For example, let's assume you're currently handling eight projects. Perhaps two of these projects are taking up the majority of your time, and the other six are moving along to one degree or another. You have other items in your pending box, as well, including plans for a business trip, and your calendar shows six meetings this week with various department heads and customers. Your tickler file contains items you have to check on at various dates to guarantee they'll be finished on time. You're also surrounded by a lot of little pieces of paper with various reminders of items that you need to do. (Or better yet, you may have a computer program or logbook you use to consolidate these reminders in one place, instead of having lots of little pieces of papers.) In other words, to keep up with everything you have to do, you really have to consult half a dozen sources. I suggest you go through all of these sources once a week. During that time, prioritize these various items and plan out your week.

WHY WEEKLY PLANNING?

Events change rapidly and it is not feasible for most people to plan a
month in advance in detail. On the other hand, if one only plans a
day in advance, there is insufficient lead time to get critical things
done. For most people, weekly planning is the most effective
planning interval.

CREATING YOUR WEEKLY ACTION PLAN

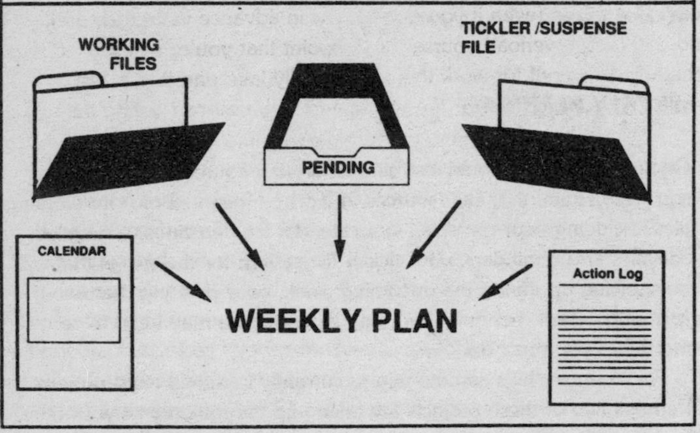

Figure 4.1. Creating your weekly plan.

Take the time to look back through your calendar to determine how
much of your time is consumed by unexpected, unplanned-for work.
Some of this will be "boss-imposed" time, when you catch the fallout
from some higher up who seems, without fail, to delegate in your
direction at the most inopportune time of the day (or week, or
month). Some of this will be, simply, unforeseen work that requires
your attention, eating up time you had intended to devote to other
work. Whatever the source, it's inevitable that at least some portion of

your day and week—perhaps 25 percent, perhaps as much as 50 percent—will be given to this type of work.

Whatever the amount, plan your work week based on the average amount of time left to you. If half of your time is used unexpectedly, you can only reasonably plan for the other 50 percent of your time to be filled with genuinely productive work of your own planning. By allowing time for the unexpected—actually the unidentified—you maintain your flexibility, you allow time for the things you know are going to crop up (even if you don't know in advance what they are), and you don't overload yourself to the point that you're actually scheduling yourself for work that would really take one and a half weeks. You've *planned for the unplanned*, and you can define the rest of your week with clarity and purpose.

By identifying and prioritizing the actions to be done in the next week, you simplify daily planning. Prioritizing is easier, too. If it's important, it will be on your weekly plan. If it isn't important, it won't be there. You only have to decide your priorities once, during your weekly planning. The advantage to this planning is that you see things in a broader context, so you can make a realistic judgment of how much time you have available to devote to various projects. You don't have to go through the whole decision-making process each time you complete a task, and that in itself takes a lot of the stress out of your work. Choosing what to do any particular day is easier. All you do is look at your calendar and note the reminders you've written down, the meetings scheduled, the work you may have scheduled for the coming week. You then take from your weekly plan list those tasks you will do that day. Figure 4.2 shows a sample weekly plan.

Setting aside time at the end of the week to do a plan for the new week makes for efficient planning time. This is not only the time to figure out what you should do but how to do it. Take time during this planning stage to think the whole thing through, to see the bigger picture. After all, most tasks are done with some larger end result in mind. With that end result in mind, you can analyze what you need to do (to have, to know) to accomplish the task.

Deciding what should be done first, second, or third, takes only a

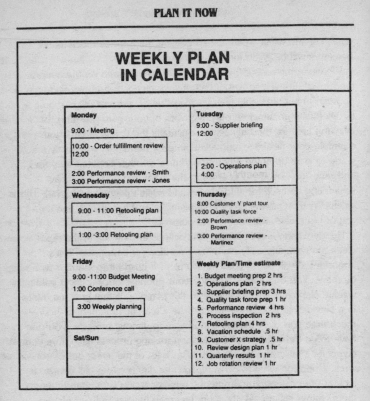

Figure 4.2. Sample weekly plan.

moment. If you schedule tasks across the work week and do your daily
planning based on the larger picture you create, you don't have to spend
time thinking about what you need to do day to day or how you're
going to do it. You have already done that as part of your weekly plan.
Instead, you can focus on the work to be done, and as you complete a
task, simply get on with doing (not just thinking about) the next one.

Whatever calendar or scheduling tool you prefer, look for one with
a "week at a glance" function. To name just a few of the options
available today, you might use a paper calendar system, any of

several types of software for desktop computers, or a handheld electronic organizer. If all the tasks for your weekly plan will actually fit in the weekly calendar view, all the better—there's far less likelihood of important things being overlooked. Figure 4.3 shows a sample weekly planning form.

It is sometimes very useful to look at your work from a broader time frame than a week. Monthly planning can provide a bird's eye view that can make weekly planning more effective. It usually consists of simply blocking out key events for the coming month. Figure 4.4 shows sample monthly planning formats.

So, what's the point of this whole weekly planning process? This is the time for you to get an overview of your job. This is the time for you to organize yourself and prepare for the new week. It's a time for you to maintain your organized state. It's a time for you to take your objectives, goals, and dreams and put them into action steps.

In his book, *How I Raised Myself from Failure to Success in Selling,* (Simon & Schuster, 1947), Frank Bettger, one of the most influential salesmen of this century, called his weekly planning time his "self-organization day." He said:

> It is surprising how much I can get done when I take enough time for planning, and it is perfectly amazing how little I get done without it. I prefer to work on a tight schedule four and half days a week and get somewhere than be working all the time and never get anywhere. (p. 25)

PROJECT IMPLEMENTATION PLANNING

In addition to the weekly planning process we've discussed, we're going to look closely at another type of planning called project planning.

We've already touched on creating your working files and how these files should represent the basic objectives and projects you're working on. Each file may represent hundreds of hours of work over a long period of time and can be pretty overwhelming.

WEEKLY PLANNING FORM

Name:_____

Week Beginning:_____

Monday	**Weekly Plan** (Consult working files, pending tray, calendar, tickler system)
	1.
	2.
Tuesday	3.
	4.
	5.
	6.
	7.
Wednesday	8.
	9.
	10.
	11.
Thursday	12.
	13.
	14.
	15.
Friday	**Unplanned activities** **added during week**
	1.
	2.
	3.
Sat/Sun	4.
	5.
	6.
	7.

Figure 4.3. Sample weekly planning form.

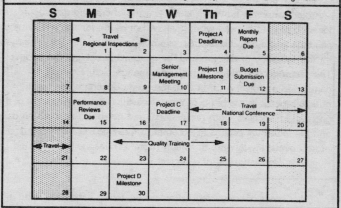

MONTHLY PLANNING FORMATS

Calendar

Monthly planning provides a bird's eye view that can make weekly planning more effective. It usually consists of simply blocking out key events for the coming month.

S	M	T	W	Th	F	S
	Travel Regional Inspections 1	2	3	Project A Deadline 4	Monthly Report Due 5	6
7	8	9	Senior Management Meeting 10	Project B Milestone 11	Budget Submission Due 12	13
14	Performance Reviews Due 15	16	Project C Deadline 17	Travel National Conference 18	19	20
Travel 21	22	Quality Training 23	24	25	26	27
28	29	Project D Milestone 30				

Figure 4.4. Sample monthly planning.

Have you ever heard the question, "How do you eat an elephant?" One fellow told me, "With lots of ketchup!" The answer, though, is one bite at a time, and this is one secret to increased productivity. If you take the time to break down larger, more complex activities into manageable and detailed tasks—as with strategic and tactical planning—you will increase your personal productivity, whether you're discussing long- or short-term goals, or multitask objectives. I cannot stress too strongly the importance of this concept when it comes to productivity and the accomplishment of work and life goals.

"Little by little does the trick"
—AESOP

Most of us know in general terms what we need to do. In fact, in my experience most of our time is consumed in considering what we need to do, thinking about how to do it, and becoming preoccupied with the details of the work involved—none of which actually accomplish anything.

Project planning, however, is the process of creating story boards for each of your life and work goals. All of us are familiar with project planning in the broad sense. An example would be the yearly budget for the company or division and the goals set to achieve the budget. The preproduction phase of making a motion picture can be considered a project plan. In fact, the preproduction phase, or the budget process, is made up of many individual project plans. All of the goals and objectives, both professional and personal, we work on daily and the individual actions to accomplish these goals can be called project plans. My favorite definition (from a colleague in the United Kingdom, Ron Hopkins) of a project is:

> [T]hat series of connected action points, which, when each and all are completed, bring into being a specific, visualized objective or result.

Each of your objectives and goals should have its own project plan.

The story board (project plan) is a set of clear mental pictures of each specific action required to move you step-by-step toward the accomplishment of the goal. Devising the project plan prompts you to explore how best to do it; in what sequence; with what resources; in how much time; with whom; and in concert with what other projects or activities need to be done.

If complete, your working files will represent each of your work objectives. A project plan should be drawn up and placed in each of your working files. Deadlines for the tasks should be noted, along with the person responsible for the task. The project plan prompts you to do things to accomplish your goals because you've visualized them clearly and analyzed the work required to accomplish them. If the tasks are defined in detail, each one can be done in short time, and accomplishing each task will result in continuous progress toward the larger objective.

When you do your weekly plan, you review each working file project plan and choose the tasks to do in the new week. You don't have to figure out over and over again what needs to be done on the project, because that part of your planning has already been done. You'll have turned your weekly planning into an efficient and speedy process that actually accomplishes what it's intended to do. Let's examine an example of this. I can't think of anything more valuable than regular, ongoing efforts toward self-improvement. In many companies this idea is reflected in an annual or semiannual job performance analysis. It's reasonable, then, that you might have a file labeled Performance Analysis in your working files. Contained in this file is your last job performance review, and in that review is your supervisor's statement that you need to do certain things over the next year to improve your performance. You've gone over this analysis with your supervisor, and you've agreed to improve your job performance.

Your Performance Analysis file should contain more than just the statement that certain things need improvement. It should contain a list of tasks you will do to accomplish these desired and *planned* improvements. You should have analyzed steps you'll proactively take to engineer improvements into yourself: books you'll read or seminars you'll attend. Or, for example, you might prepare a checklist you use daily or weekly to overcome a tendency to be too casual about record keeping. And you'll pull that task list out once a week and read through it with real intent.

When you read through your task list, ask yourself what you've done this week, or today, or this afternoon about a particular area of weakness. Ask yourself what task you can do. Turn to next week's page in your calendar system and list the specific tasks for the week from the already-created project plan that will move that particular self-improvement project forward.

A sample project plan is shown in Figure 4.5

PROJECT IMPLEMENTATION PLANNING

SAMPLE PROJECT IMPLEMENTATION PLAN

Project Title: Office Procedures Manual

Objective: To develop office procedures that have the support of management and staff by the first half of this year.

ACTIONS	Estimated Hours	People Involved	Target Date	Completion Date
1. Collect current procedures	2	Assistant	1 / 15	
2. Establish task forces to review current procedures and needed changes	4	Self	1 / 20	
3. Task forces review procedures and submit recommendations*	*	Task Force	2 / 5	
4. Read and synthesize recommendations	3	Self	2 /15	
5. Review by legal counsel		Counsel	2 / 20	
6. Circulate draft for comment by managers		Readers	3 / 1	
7. Make final edits	3	Self	3 / 5	
8. Oversee production*	*	Assistant	3 / 15	
9. Write project plan for internal PR campaign to encourage use	1	Self	3 / 20	
10. Distribute manual	2	Assistant	4 / 20	
DUE DATE: 5 / 1 / 95				

* Those assigned task should each develop their own project implementation plan to break this task down

Figure 4.5. Sample project implementation plan.

CRITERIA FOR PROJECT PLANNING

Some criteria you can use to determine if work you need to do falls into the category of project planning follows:

- It is complex.
- It seems difficult.
- It involves several staff.

- It is a new activity.
- There are critical deadlines.
- You are coping with changes.

IMPLEMENTATION MAPPING

At times you will need to give thought to the design of a project plan before you can work out the implementation steps. Implementation mapping (Figure 4.6) helps identify the critical elements in the project plan, generating pertinent ideas in a free-flowing process, triggering thoughts that otherwise might lie hidden.

The key elements of implementation mapping are:

- Brainstorm about all elements of the task.
- Identify the critical elements to success.
- Group ideas into categories.
- Incorporate these into an implementation plan.

PLANNING ON A COMPUTER

I do my planning on a computer. I use a Lotus software product and have designed an application called PEP Planner for Windows that makes it easy to do a project plan. All the forms I need and the structure or format I prefer have been created in a macro command that requires only a few simple keystrokes to see my tasks and all the information I need from many different points of view.

I can add a task into the project plan, along with a due date and the name of the person responsible for the task completion, and this information automatically shows up in my calendar. This way, I only have to write the information down once, yet I can retrieve it several ways—by due date, by project plan designation, by the name of the person responsible or whatever is most convenient for me at the moment.

I can do my weekly plans quickly, and a computer function lets me highlight the project plan tasks I want to accomplish during the coming

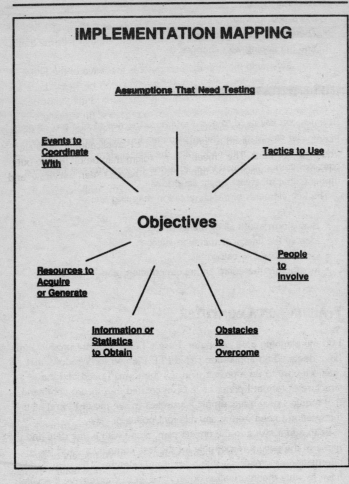

IMPLEMENTATION MAPPING

Assumptions That Need Testing

Events to Coordinate With

Tactics to Use

Objectives

People to Involve

Resources to Acquire or Generate

Information or Statistics to Obtain

Obstacles to Overcome

Figure 4.6. Implementation mapping.

week. As I write this, for example, my computer is tracking 1,568 tasks I have to do. I know that because the computer tells me that's how many tasks I have to do.

Group planning through the computer is the wave of the future. I don't have to tell you how wasteful meetings can be, yet today's paradigm is that you hold a meeting if you want to get things done. Now we have inexpensive tools to link up groups (in virtually any location) and ways to discuss, plan, and track those plans through the computer. I've devised a "groupware" PEP application to facilitate doing exactly this. The "meeting" paradigm may be on its way out. There may be ways to do things that we haven't seen until now, and the way we do things in the future will be dramatically altered.

Already some of you are digging your heels in, ready to resist the idea of using a computer for planning and managing your work and your group's work. I can honestly tell you, though, that in the years ahead you'll either make the maximum use of computers or die professionally. We really have very little choice in the matter. People have to learn to see computers as tools (just as a pen or pencil is a tool) and realize that they can control and monitor and produce much better with a computer than without. No doubt, you would agree technology is having a profound effect on our personal and professional lives and will continue to do so. You cannot expect to see the possibilities technology might bring to you and your business unless you *use* technology. You will find, using technology to plan will not only encourage more and better planning, it will also enable you to see more ways to incorporate technology into your business.

Again, why all this trouble? Because we all want to succeed. In the book *Think and Grow Rich* (Ballantine Books, 1960), Napoleon Hill studied Andrew Carnegie, Henry Ford, and others. One of the common denominators shared by these successful people was that they were meticulous planners. Each knew what he/she wanted to accomplish. Each took the time to figure out how to accomplish his goals and then worked until he did exactly that. It's a model we all need to follow.

STRATEGIC PLANNING

With a daily, weekly, and project plan we have identified the tactical steps necessary to get things done. But the question remains, are you getting the things done you should be getting done? Have you chosen the right projects to do? Do you have the long-term view in mind? Are the projects based on a sound assessment of where you should be headed? Are they the efforts that will get you where you want to go in the most effective and efficient way? Do you have the resources to carry out these grand plans or could the resources be used more wisely?

Strategy is all wrapped up in goals and, finally, what is important to the business or you. Without a clear long-term vision, whatever you may be able to get done in a day or week, a year, or a lifetime may not get you very far or be all that valuable.

You must be working on the right thing. I have worked with hundreds of companies over the years and although some may have developed strategies for their business or division, few of the staff have any clue of what these strategies are. Defining the strategies to be followed and making them known allows all staff members to better align their own individual actions with the important objectives of the group.

How do you develop a strategy? This is easily the subject of a book on its own. First you must establish the goals you wish to attain. These goals will be driven by your vision and your customers' needs. (More on this later in this chapter under GOAL SETTING and VALUES.) Where are you now in respect to these goals? How do you get from where you are now to where you want to go? What resources do you have to work with (finances, people, time, knowledge, experience, contacts who have solved the problems you face in accomplishing your goals, and so forth)? What is the best use of existing resources to get you to where you want to go? Give yourself a direction. Consider the variables. Think the thought through as far as you possibly can.

In some companies, the development of the strategy is part of the yearly budget process. This may be too narrow a focus. Yes, finances are a critical resource (and restraint). But financial goals and the strategic planning for achieving them is only one part of the process. Linking strategic review so closely to the budget process review may prevent you from seeing the value and relation of strategic planning process to other areas of the business.

Strategic planning, as I view it, is a tool for any job level. Any objective or goal should have a strategy developed for its accomplishment. The overall strategy of the activity should be used to guide the individual in the development of his or her own strategies. With a good strategy in place, establishing the priorities to be worked on is easy. Establishing the ingredients—what working files need to be created and which of these working files requires a project—is also much easier. The question now becomes, what to strategize?

> *"If you don't know where you are going, any road will get you there."*
> —UNKNOWN

GOAL SETTING

Strategies are built around goals. A goal is a timeless and broad objective or aim, the end to which efforts and actions are directed. An objective might be defined as an aim set against time.

Goals can be made up of numerous objectives. These objectives would be determined as part of the strategic planning process. An example of a strategic goal might be to become the largest manufacturer of toothbrushes in Spain. An example of a strategic objective might be to increase market share this year from 10 percent to 15 percent.

With goals come meaning. Without goals, there is little or no meaning in work and life, and without meaning there can only be dissatisfaction and a general unhappiness. A goal acts as a guiding light. It sets direction. But it isn't enough to have a vague idea of your goals. Goals must be well defined, preferably worked out in writing. It's one thing to think about something; it's another to write it down. Writing forces you to clarify your thoughts.

To ensure you have a complete set of goals, you must first define the different parts of your work. In his book, *The 7 Habits of Highly Effective People* (Simon & Schuster, 1989), Stephen Covey refers to the various roles people play. Marketing manager, chairman of the credit committee, XYZ board member, quality circle leader, staff trainer, can all be considered staff roles you play. Each part of your work life or role you have to play will have its own set of goals. When you see how many goals come into play, it isn't hard to see why people may have difficulty achieving them, particularly if you lack the system required to accomplish your goals.

PERSONAL GOALS

We've all known someone who talked on and on about some fantasy, such as giving it all up and moving to Tahiti. Suppose a person fantasizes for years about moving to Tahiti, but it isn't meant to be. It is too expensive; he never has the time or money; or his job eats up every moment of his life. It's sad that so many people live their lives without realizing their dreams.

At least in this example, the person had a dream, but the dreamer didn't know how to achieve it. Maybe it was too overwhelming. Or maybe the dream was too dreamlike—it never became a clearly defined goal where objectives could be identified and set against real time.

Once you define your personal roles—mother or father, wife or husband, self, friend, volunteer, golfer—make sure each role has its own goals, defined and written down.

Whether personal or professional, goals function like directional lights. They shed light on overriding objectives and provide us a reason to develop strategies. Still, we need to know that our goals are important and meaningful. What your goals are depends on what you value.

VALUES

While most business is conducted to create profit, long-term success requires more than achieving that one goal. For example, you might improve current profit by eliminating investment toward the future or by cutting costs to the detriment of customer service, but either activity could mean the death of the business.

It is the responsibility of the top executives to define what is truly important to the business. This is not some PR exercise. It is a serious strategic step. What is the reason for the existence of your business? What principles does the business live by? What is your organizational vision? What are the governing values of the business?

Often a company defines its purpose and principles in a one-page mission statement and invites employees to develop goals and objectives in alignment with it.

As a manager you might call together your management team to delineate the most important issues your department (group, or business) is facing, where you want the business to be in the next several years, and what might prevent you from being there. You might involve all of your staff in the process. The end result would be agreement on the most important issues to deal with so business and professional goals can be met.

VALUES ON A PERSONAL LEVEL

The most important question you can ask yourself is "What truly matters to me? What principles should I live by?" If you determine what your principles are—those ideals that you value above all else—your purpose or mission in life becomes all the more clear. If you know what is important to you, you can then establish goals to realize it. These goals will be meaningful, because achieving them will give you what you truly value.

There is tremendous strength in this approach. Charles R. Hobbs, the author of the book *Time Power* (Harper & Row, 1987), calls this self-unification:

> *When what you do is in congruity with what you believe, and what you believe is the highest of truths, you achieve the most gratifying form of personal productivity and experience the most satisfying form of self-esteem. (p. 21)*

By establishing your most vital priorities in life you can achieve what Hobbs describes as a concentration of power: "the ability to focus on and accomplish your most vital priorities."

Establishing your values isn't a glib exercise. You're reading this book because you appreciate how valuable time is. You no doubt want more control of it. You want to be able to make better use of it. It would be a shame to come to the end of your life and realize you had not done and been what you wanted to do and be.

Dr. Wayne Dyer, in his audio tape series, *Real Magic*, talks of his experiences working in a hospital with terminally ill patients. He noticed that no one ever regretted not having spent more time in the office. The regrets were about the handling of relationships or time with loved ones.

Don't wait until it's too late to realize you have spent the bulk of the time of your life on things that were not the most important to you. It's far better to analyze your goals, your beliefs, and your guiding principles and to make sure your work is in alignment with them.

Most of us want happiness in life. But what brings it about? Happiness is a by-product of working and living with meaning and purpose. Establishing goals based on one's values provides that meaning and a purpose for living. The beauty of working toward the accomplishment of a goal is that it almost doesn't matter whether you achieve the goal or not—the fact that you are working toward things that matter to you is enough to bring you happiness. Even the most mundane of actions becomes tolerable, even enjoyable, because you know it's leading you closer to the accomplishment of your goals.

If you're to do the things that are most important to you in life, you will need to manage your time wisely:

- Decide what you value above all else.
- Decide what principles you wish to live by.
- Identify your mission in life.

VISUALIZATION—WHAT YOU SEE IS WHAT YOU GET

You're most likely familiar with the concept of visualizing desired results before the actual performance. Athletes have employed the technique for years. Visualization means crossing the finish line in your mind's eye or imagining the perfect dive. Everything slows down, and you're aware of all that is happening. You see yourself making that three-point basket in the final game of the NBA championship playoffs, just as the buzzer sounds to win the game. Charles Garfield, a research psychologist, has spent many years studying hundreds of world-class athletes. In his book *Peak Performance: Mental Training Techniques of the World's Greatest Athletes* (Warner Books, 1984), he says:

> *All peak performers I have interviewed report that they use some form of mental rehearsal in both training and competition.*

How important is organizational vision? Jim Clemmer, in his book, *Firing On All Cylinders* (Irwin Professional Publishers, 1992), writes:

> *Your organizational vision acts as a magnet. It attracts people, events, and circumstances to it. Another way of looking at visioning is as a self-fulfilling prophecy. What your people believe will happen, they will make happen, often unconsciously.*

We've spoken of action following clarity of picture. The planning process described in this chapter allows you to get that clarity of picture. There is a difference between "dreaming about having something in the future" and "*visualizing* having it in the future."

Visualizing implies a more structured and disciplined view of what you are trying to accomplish. By visualizing, you look at your goal from many different viewpoints. By examining your work from all of the viewpoints described here, you get clarity and act on the things that are the most important and will result in the greatest payback.

By dreaming and visualizing (prompted by a good planning process), you create more reasons to want what you are looking at and you increase your desire for it. Want and desire, in no small part, determine whether you accomplish what you set out for.

The Japanese are known for the speed by which they can bring a new product to the market. Yet they also have a reputation for taking a long time to decide. This has been incorrectly labeled as a Japanese process of consensus building. Yes, they build consensus. But they also make sure that every angle has been thoroughly looked at before they begin. And once they begin, they act with blinding speed.

You must go through this thorough process if you are to act in the most effective way. The planning process prompts you to examine your work from many points of view. You identify the objects that comprise the objective—the work. The work is categorized in many additional ways it might not otherwise be if you neglected thorough planning.

You must be well organized to execute this all-essential planning process efficiently. You don't necessarily want to spend a lot of time on it. You want to spend the vast amount of time getting the actions done. But the time and effort are worth it. When you learn to plan most effectively, you'll discover that you are spending some part of every day visualizing and, better yet, *actualizing* your goals with this process.

FOLLOW-UP FOR CHAPTER 4

1. Commit to a daily and weekly action plan. With practice, a weekly analysis of your work for the coming week should take you two to four hours on Friday and probably less if you computerize the process. Devote ten minutes or so to a daily action plan each morning of the work week and track your progress through the work day. Your daily planning will be much simplified if you "work backward," from the larger picture of a weekly plan and derive your daily To Do lists from a series of tasks designed to move you closer to a larger goal.

2. As part of your weekly action plan, go through all of your sources of work. Prioritize these various items and plan out your week. Eliminate multiple sources by combining any stray notes into one list. Use these current notations, along with items in your pending box and tickler file, to create your weekly list.

3. Remember to allow sufficient time in your planning for unplanned or unidentified work.

4. Remember to define the key objectives to be accomplished. Break down these objectives into smaller tasks to be accomplished. Once a week, review these activities, and use them to help create a weekly action plan for yourself. These projects should be counted among your sources of work identified in step 2 above.

5. Define what is important to the business in the long term. Where do you want the business (or your portion, area of responsibility) to be in the years ahead? You may invite your staff to participate in this process. From this process define specifically (and in writing) what goals you will work on over a defined period of time.

6. Create a working file for each goal.

7. Establish a strategy for the accomplishment of each goal.

8. Write project plans covering the tactical steps necessary to accomplish the strategies.

9. Apply this same process to your personal life, if you are so inclined.

Follow Up and Follow Through

When you get right down to the root of the meaning of the word succeed, you find that it simply means to follow through.
—F. W. NICHOL

Chapter 5 Preview

In this chapter, you will learn:

- Persistence is the most vital ingredient of success in life and work.
- To put the right systems in place to allow you to remember details.
- To use a calendar and other tools to follow up and follow through.
- To practice effective delegation. Unlimited growth is possible only through eliciting the support of others.

In Chapter 4 we covered how essential it is to have an efficient planning process in place if you are to realize your goals and objectives. Planning gives clarity and with clarity you act. But how successful and effective you are will most depend on how well you stick to what you are trying to accomplish; in other words, how well you follow up and follow through.

PERSISTENCE

When I say stick to it, I almost literally mean it. Things get done, objectives are met, goals are achieved most often because the person who wanted them stuck to it and made them happen. Calvin Coolidge, the former president of the United States said:

Nothing in the world can take the place of persistence. Talent will not; nothing is more common than unsuccessful men with talent. Genius will not; unrewarded genius is almost a proverb. Education will not; the world is full of educated derelicts. Persistence and determination alone are omnipotent.

I suspect that your experience tells you this is true. Things happen because you make them happen, and/or persist until they do. Planning's relationship to persistence can best be summed up in a quote of Napoleon Hill in his book, *Think and Grow Rich* (Fawcett Books, 1960). He said:

The majority of men meet with failure because of their lack of persistence in creating new plans to take the place of those which fail.

This is the essence of the work process. Know what you want. Plan how to get it. Act on the plans. Follow up until it happens, or develop new plans to make it happen. Follow up on the new plans over and over until you achieve what you want. How well you do it is determined by how well you are organized.

By following the steps of the Personal Efficiency Program (PEP), you've become action oriented. You *Do It Now*. You've organized your work space and you have systems in place to keep it that way. You know how to set goals and plan to achieve them. These same principles must be applied to how you follow up and follow through.

FORGET REMEMBERING

Most people I speak with take a certain degree of pride in their ability to remember "everything" that needs to be done. It is a mental game they play. While that may have been okay at one time, the pace of today's work and home life and the volume of activities we could or should keep up with have grown so much that it is impractical to expect to keep on top of 1,000 things to do. No doubt you do remember these things to do, but it may not be at the time it's most convenient or effective, such as at 3:00 in the morning, when you sit up in bed and think, "Oh, I have to take care of. . . ." This constant thinking about, planning out, tracking everything you need to do—remembering everything you need to follow up on—simply overwhelms people.

I don't believe that you necessarily want to reinforce this ability to remember the many hundreds of details that make up your workload. Executives and managers should be more interested in forgetting about all these things they need to do. Yes, I said forgetting. What people need is the right system in place, to allow them to remember this myriad of details when, and only when, it's necessary for them to remember.

Sounds crazy? Not really.

It has been said that Albert Einstein couldn't tell you his own telephone number. When asked why, he was reported to have said, "Why should I know it? I can always find it in the directory."

PREOCCUPATION AND TIME

Have you ever noticed the first time you drive someplace it seems to take longer to get there than the second or third time? Have you ever considered why? The first time you drive somewhere you tend to be alert to where you are and where you are going. You are on the lookout for landmarks. "Three blocks past the pharmacy on Hilton Street" forces you to keep an eye out for the pharmacy and count the blocks. Once you have been there a few times, you can drive there hardly noticing the lights that go by. You get in the car and the next thing you know you are there! The sense of time has little to do with how fast you are driving. It has much more to do with how alert you are. Anyone driving today can agree that too many people driving are in their own mental world. They are preoccupied.

When you are preoccupied time flies by. You will have experienced starting the workday only to discover it is time for lunch and you wonder where the morning went and what you accomplished. Too often the cause of this preoccupation is our attempt to make sense of and keep up with the thousands of things we must do. It is the result of a poor planning process. It is our attempt to keep on top of all the things we must track and do, *mentally*.

I am convinced that this constant, unproductive preoccupation with all the things we have to do is the single largest consumer of time and energy, the biggest barrier to individual productivity, and the one thing we can all do something about to materially allow us to take control of our time and our work, and therefore our lives.

ORGANIZE EFFICIENT FOLLOW-UP SYSTEMS

All too often when I arrive at someone's desk, I find it scattered with
reminders of things to do, perhaps in the form of Post-It notes spread
out on the computer screen and over every imaginable surface. Even
if you have a strong *Do It Now* habit, there are normally many things
you can't complete at the moment for one reason or another.
Accordingly, people leave themselves reminders.

However, having those reminders constantly staring you in the face
isn't necessarily conducive to concentration, focus, and productivity. If
these little reminders linger long enough one eventually becomes blind
to them. Regularly looking at all of these reminders and consciously
deciding not to do any one of them reinforces a *Don't Do It Now*
habit.

Having simple and easy reminder systems (tools) in place enable
you to overcome these problems and move on to your most
important work.

Paper Follow-Up

Since paper is so abundant and one of the biggest nuisances around,
let's begin by discussing how to handle paper. You know it's possible
to get the papers off of your desk and "forwarded" to an appropriate
time to do them. You can do this with a tickler file system that lets
you schedule materials by the days of the month (1 through 31), or
by months (1 through 12), according to due dates.

As we discussed in Chapter 2, simply make a reminder for yourself
in your calendar, and then block out time to do the work. Put the
reminder—the piece of paper you'll actually be working on—into the
tickler system on the same date you scheduled in your calendar, so it
will pop up on the day you scheduled for it. Put papers that are
awaiting someone else's input into the tickler system. For example, if
you send a letter to a customer and expect to hear back within a
week, put your copy of the letter into the tickler system. After a week,

your copy of the letter pops up, prompting you to get back to the customer for more follow-up. If a response has been received, the response will dictate your next step. Either way, the reminder prompts you to follow up and follow through.

One clever and successful man ran a medium-size bank using just this system. He had a tickler system numbered 1–31 and 1–12. This one follow-up tool was used and the whole management of the bank could be traced. He would assign duties and tasks to people or write down things to be done and use the tickler system to anticipate when he thought an assignment or a project could reasonably (and efficiently) be completed. When the reminder popped up at a date in the future, he followed up and followed through.

Logbook

Consolidating all the small tasks you need to do in one book eliminates the need for little pieces of paper littering your desk. A logbook of such items makes a useful reminder tool for the "odds and ends" of work that are part of everyone's day. You can use it when you suddenly remember something you need to do and want a place to write it down. Colleagues may pass by and verbally ask you to check on something and get back to them on it; the logbook gives you a place to write down the request and a means to note your follow-up, all in one.

I recommend a composition notebook, probably about 6 by 9½ inches in size. Not a spiral-bound notebook. Use a stitched book so the pages cannot be easily ripped out. In it maintain a chronological diary of activities. You should date each entry. Write big, and put a straight line between each entry, so you can easily distinguish between tasks. As you complete a task, put a big X through it (see Figure 5.1). This lets you see what's been done and what remains to be done.

One manager ran his entire business using this one tool. Everything he needed to remember went into his personal logbook. He took it wherever he went.

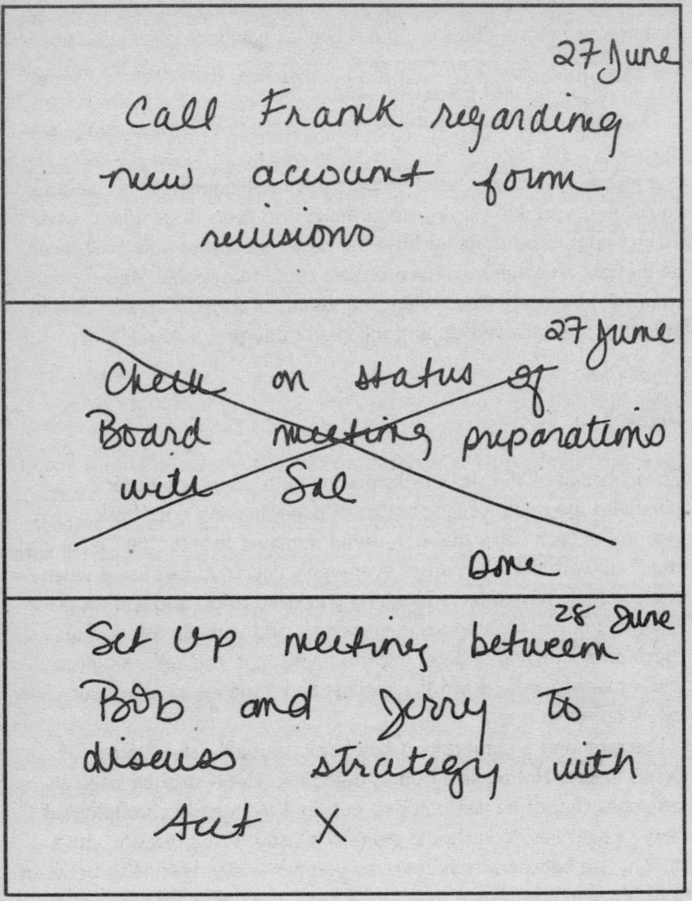

27 June

Call Frank regarding new account form revisions

27 June

Check on status of Board meeting preparations with Sal

Done

28 June

Set Up meeting between Bob and Jerry to discuss strategy with Act X

Figure 5.1. Sample entries in a logbook.

Simply using a logbook to organize and remember things to do can be an effective reminder system, especially for secretaries. In fact, nearly all professional secretaries I have worked with have had some form of logbook.

Until you get used to writing everything down in it I recommend you always leave it open on your desk. Otherwise, chances are you will reach for the closest thing to write on and you won't develop the habit of using your logbook.

Calendar Systems

Even if you use a logbook, you will always need some form of calendar system. There are many calendar systems on the market. The Franklin Planner, Day-Timers organizer system, and Time Manager International calendaring system and course are but a few of the many calendar systems you may have seen. Each of these has a built-in philosophy of time management. These planners are excellent follow-up tools. After all, you can be reasonably sure you'll check your calendar daily, so it makes a good place to jot down items you want to remember. Because calendars are dated, they anticipate future needs, and you can use them as a sort of linear tickler file, if nothing else.

Our Scandinavian offices have designed calendar systems following the planning concepts of PEP. Like others mentioned here, this is a calendar system you can carry around with you (fits in a small purse or suit pocket for convenience and use it to track your activities and plan your week. It has a week-at-a-glance calendar view and sections for addresses and telephone numbers, as well as other personal information.)

One good rule of thumb for any calendar system is this: Whether you choose a large, desk-bound calendar system with many sections and features or a simple calendar system you carry in your purse or suit pocket, use one with a week-at-a-glance feature. This will reinforce your likelihood to plan on a weekly and a week-long basis

and increase your chances of success in both scheduling and
accomplishing your work.

If you're inclined to use a bigger and more sophisticated system,
you might include sections such as an address book section, a section
for your project plans, or a section for notes you take during meetings.
Learn to use your calendar system to its full potential. A little
imagination, combined with the necessary training and trial and error,
will show you follow-up and follow-through capabilities.

Besides keeping track of appointments, calendars hold a wealth of
important information, including

- Reminders of future tasks.
- To Do lists or plans for the upcoming week.
- Important deadlines.
- Birthdays, holidays, anniversaries, and other special dates.
- A place to write notes from meetings.
- Address and telephone information.
- General information, such as time zones, area codes, and weights,
  measures, and equivalents.
- Blocked out time for scheduled work.
- Scheduled time for recurring activities such as weekly meetings
  with your employees or processing your E-mail or paperwork.
- Personal information such as insurance numbers, driver's license
  number, and auto registration number.
- Pockets for storing receipts for reimbursements or deductions.

A well-used calendar for scheduling and following through on
activities might look as shown in Figure 5.2.

Electronic Solutions to Follow-Up and Follow-Through

Getting more use out of your existing calendar or upgrading to a
bigger, more sophisticated calendar is a simple refinement of an
existing process that you probably already have in place. Should you

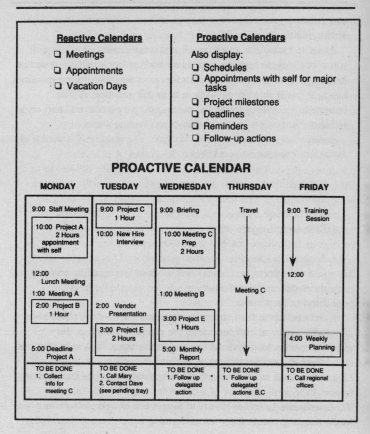

Reactive Calendars
- ❏ Meetings
- ❏ Appointments
- ❏ Vacation Days

Proactive Calendars

Also display:
- ❏ Schedules
- ❏ Appointments with self for major tasks
- ❏ Project milestones
- ❏ Deadlines
- ❏ Reminders
- ❏ Follow-up actions

PROACTIVE CALENDAR

MONDAY	TUESDAY	WEDNESDAY	THURSDAY	FRIDAY
9:00 Staff Meeting	9:00 Project C 1 Hour	9:00 Briefing	Travel	9:00 Training Session
10:00 Project A 2 Hours appointment with self	10:00 New Hire Interview	10:00 Meeting C Prep 2 Hours		
12:00 Lunch Meeting				12:00
1:00 Meeting A		1:00 Meeting B	Meeting C	
2:00 Project B 1 Hour	2:00 Vendor Presentation	3:00 Project E 1 Hours		
	3:00 Project E 2 Hours			4:00 Weekly Planning
5:00 Deadline Project A		5:00 Monthly Report		
TO BE DONE 1. Collect info for meeting C	TO BE DONE 1. Call Mary 2. Contact Dave (see pending tray)	TO BE DONE 1. Follow up delegated action	TO BE DONE 1. Follow up delegated actions B,C	TO BE DONE 1. Call regional offices

Figure 5.2. Sample calendar for scheduling and follow-up.

wish to make a more dramatic change in your working life, you might consider one of the many electronic systems on the market.

Technology is quickly catching up to and matching the needs of virtually every individual. There are handheld calendar systems not much bigger or heavier than Day-Timers or other notebook-type calendar systems that can provide us with vast amounts of information. Coming down the scale, the size we associated with "desktop" ten years ago is now "palm size" in the world of computers.

Whatever the size, there are some drawbacks. A palm-size computer/calendar system may have a keyboard that's difficult to work with. But even that question is being addressed now, with devotees using narrow stylus-type instruments to key in their information and requests. There are even computers the size of an ordinary ink pen today. The technology is still in its infancy and the cost may be prohibitive for some of us, but soon the cost will come down and the technology will leapfrog yet another generation. These trends indicate that these "electronic organizers" will increase in popularity and will certainly challenge paper-based systems for superiority (and popularity) in the future.

Meanwhile, we at the Institute for Business Technology (IBT) have designed a personal computer software program based on the planning and tracking systems covered in this book. The software, called PEP Planner for Windows, outlines the process for better self-organization and so addresses the problems most people face in trying to plan their work. The use of a computer and PEP Planner for Windows software makes it easy to keep track of everything you need to do, allowing you to focus on performing work instead of worrying about it.

In the past, learning how to use a software program could have been difficult. But organizing yourself with this software is fast and flexible. Instead of the tedious and sometimes time-consuming effort that goes into planning on paper, PEP Planner for Windows lets you use your computer to jot things down quickly and then revise your plans according to your needs with just a few keystrokes. You can see at a glance what you have to do on each project. And it's easy to rearrange, add, or delete steps without rewriting each affected item or each plan out all over again as you do when you plan on paper.

You can also plant reminders for future dates that will automatically (electronically) pop up at the appropriate time. You can store frequently used information literally at your fingertips, keep track of appointments and meetings, and keep files safely stored in your computer. To make organizing easy, PEP Planner for Windows provides easy-access call-up screens, so all you have to do is type in the requested function: Calendar, logbook, yearly planner, people (batch) section, pending tasks section, preset project files, address book, and so forth.

An electronic solution such as the PEP Planner for Windows takes a lot of the work out of planning for you by automatically batching activities and key words. Instead of thumbing through a tickler file, wondering where you put this or that, you can retrieve all pertinent information for a project with a search function by typing in the assigned project name or the name of the client it concerns, and the computer will search until it finds it.

To track your work and to organize yourself I recommend either the PEP Planner for Windows or a comparable personal information manager (PIM) software application.

Combination Paper and Electronic Calendaring Systems

Although I usually encourage people to embrace technology and computerize their calendaring systems, some may find that computerization doesn't fit their type of work or they cannot afford such tools. For example, going to a lunch appointment with a laptop computer may be a bit much. Many people successfully combine paper and electronic calendaring systems, taking advantage of both. Most electronic PIM software packages can print out your calendar in almost any conceivable size. When going to appointments you can use a printout.

Relatively inexpensive handheld computers with built-in software can keep track of essential personal information (addresses, things to do, calendaring features) without all the elaborate functions of laptops or notebook computers. Handheld computers fit easily into a purse or suit pocket. Meanwhile, you can maintain your paper system to outline your project plans and have the bulk of your reference materials in your desk or briefcase.

WORK GROUPS

With the advent of network systems it is now possible and even affordable to network nearly any group within an organization. What used to require a million dollar investment is now affordable for most small groups. The hardware and software needed to network and communicate with each other is affordable to virtually every business.

Follow-up and follow-through is greatly enhanced in a group setting, of course, because groups can develop specific plans for a variety of projects involving any number of different people. These plans can be implemented concurrently, tracked, supervised, or merely viewed by any member of the group.

From the manager's perspective, multiple projects can be tracked with ease. You can view any one or all of the projects your direct reports are responsible for. You can also view the separate tasks and completion deadlines for any of those projects or view the separate (and multiple) tasks for more than one project simultaneously, depending on your software and hardware. This capability lets you keep track of multiple deadlines.

You can get a perspective on the work being done from the viewpoint of any of the people involved and track work that needs to be completed concurrently or prior to the completion of other assignments. You can identify problems you may have been unaware of or, at best, merely suspected. For example, if you view the task list of several of your people in columns on a single screen and you see one has an unfair or overly large task load, you may want to look again at how your office delegates.

As changes, modifications, or updates are made, everyone in the network automatically has those updates available to them. Information can be viewed against time and deadlines. If an individual becomes ill, it's easy to identify his or her responsibilities and tasks, and then redistribute them equitably among the other members of the group. The need for physically meeting to cover issues or plans is greatly reduced, thereby increasing the time available for actual work.

If you truly want to reengineer how you work, you must consider work group software and information exchange through a PC network. IBT has developed its own special software applications that can be used in work groups following the PEP principles.

FOLLOW-UP AND DELEGATION

Delegation determines to a large degree your effectiveness as an executive, manager, or supervisor. The quality of your work also depends on your ability to properly delegate. Proper delegation enables you to follow up and follow through effectively. If you delegate properly, you will multiply your productivity.

The sooner in your planning process that you detect overload—yours or someone else's—the more effective you will be if you correct the problem. You can't expect to do everything yourself.

You can waste a lot of time trying to master something you are not very good at. Delegating properly, to the right person with the right skills, is one of the most important executive skills. When you delegate, you are assigning another person a task to do and the authority to do it, even though you do not hand over your personal accountability. That stays with you.

One of the best sources of information on the subject of delegation is the book *Don't Do. Delegate!* (Ballantine Books, 1985) by James Jenks and John Kelly. The following two lists, gleaned from this and other sources, contrast effective and ineffective delegation.

The Effective Delegator

1. Identifies the correct person to do the job.
2. Delegates now, giving adequate time for completion.
3. Clearly states the objective.
4. Provides all information needed to complete the task.
5. Makes sure staff understands a task before they take action.
6. Sets deadline for completion.
7. Encourages written project plan.
8. Regularly monitors progress.
9. Is accessible for clarification and advice.
10. Assumes responsibility, but gives credit to the person who did the job.
11. Helps staff grow by introducing them to new responsibilities.

The Ineffective Delegator

1. Distributes workload arbitrarily.
2. Delegates just before deadline, thereby creating crisis.
3. Does not clearly communicate the envisioned outcome.
4. Issues minimal, hurried instructions.
5. Delegates in a way that creates misunderstandings.
6. Asks for everything as soon as possible.
7. Hopes staff develops an effective approach to task.
8. Establishes no formal review process.
9. Interferes with how job is being done.
10. Assigns blame to others if result not achieved but takes credit if achieved.
11. Doesn't delegate but instead holds on to the task and acts as a bottleneck.

There is a more important reason to refine your skills of getting others to do the work for you. Eliciting the support of others is the only way you will achieve broad success, both personally and professionally. Only by tapping into the support of others can you multiply your output. There is a limit to any one individual's productive capacity, time, and knowledge. Skillful delegation means limitless production potential.

EXCEPTIONS TO THE RULE

It can be very frustrating when you have to track down what others have done. On the other hand, if you don't track your subordinates' work, it often means failure. How you pass on things to others to do can affect your results. Effective delegation greatly increases your chances of success. Some people simply will not perform, don't delegate to them. Give the job to someone else or figure out another way to do get the job done.

I use an old rule of thumb. When it comes to getting something done, *give it to a busy person.* Idle people often remain idle when given things to do. Busy people—if they are effective—are busy because they are consistently and regularly working, and that's the person you want to assign tasks to.

> *Next week there can't be any crisis. My schedule*
> *is already full.*
> —HENRY A. KISSINGER

BACK UP YOUR SYSTEMS

In a movie entitled *Taking Care of Business* the character played by actor Charles Grodin leaves his calendar system in a phone booth at an airport and it is found by a convict who has escaped from prison. The movie is a comedy and produces lots of laughs about this poor guy's experiences, but it also drives home how much we depend on our follow-up and reminder systems.

The chances of misplacing your calendar system or having your computer malfunction are high. I back up my hard drive on floppy disks each week when I create my weekly plan.

A colleague of mine makes copies of his paper calendar system. Not necessarily the entire calendar but all of the personal information, addresses, telephone numbers, and so forth. He was once very grateful to have done so. He misplaced his original but because of the copy, he found it relatively painless to reconstruct the information.

If you are susceptible to forgetting things, you should make sure you regularly back up your reminder system so that it will be there when you need it.

MAKE FOLLOW-UP PART OF THE WORK PROCESS

Your weekly planning process becomes the formal time for you to get an overview of your work, look at all of your objectives and plans, prioritize your upcoming week, and remind yourself of what you need to follow up on. Scheduling your weekly planning and doing it ensures that no important item gets overlooked.

As an executive, manager, or supervisor, your weekly one-to-one meeting with your direct reports is the time to follow up on the items you're tracking through to completion. By scheduling and holding these meetings regularly, your people know what to expect. They know it is time for progress reports and that progress is expected. It eliminates random checking and disturbing your people in the process. Your staff members, in turn, have the chance to follow up with you on input you're expected to supply. They know the meeting is predictable, useful time that helps them get their own jobs done better and faster.

If you learn to recognize the tools that exist to facilitate follow-up and follow-through and make these tools an efficient part of the work process, you'll make it much easier to persist to success.

FOLLOW-UP FOR CHAPTER 5

1. How successful and effective you are primarily depends on how well you stick to what you're trying to accomplish, in other words, how well you follow up and follow through. Things happen because you make them happen, or you must persist until you do.

2. Adopt simple and easy reminder systems that will enable you to overcome problems and let you move on to your most important work. If you have a stack of papers on your desk that detail tasks to be done, eliminate the clutter by scheduling this work in your calendar, and filing the papers in a tickler file. Then, on the appropriate date, the papers will be there to remind you of a task to be done, and you will have blocked out the time to complete that task.

3. Eliminate the clutter of multiple reminders by consolidating everything into a logbook. Use it everyday to reinforce the habit, and you'll keep your desk clear at the same time. Use the logbook when you suddenly remember something you need to do and you want a place to write it down. Use it to keep track of verbal requests to do things. Date each task to be done, and cross off the task when it's completed. A logbook provides a reminder system and a follow-up system all in one by prompting you to do things and verifying tasks that have been completed.

4. Use a calendar system that lets you plan an entire week at a time. This will reinforce your likelihood to plan on a weekly and a week-long basis and increase your chances of success in both scheduling and accomplishing your work.

5. Learn not to limit the use of your calendar system. People almost never use a calendar system to its full potential. A little imagination, combined with the necessary trial and error, will show you follow-up and follow-through capabilities you never anticipated.

6. Don't overlook electronic solutions to your problems. Handheld, computerized calendar systems are available that aren't much bigger or heavier than Day-Timers or other notebook-type calendar systems and can provide you with vast amounts of information. Trends indicate that these electronic organizers will increase in popularity and will certainly challenge paper-based systems for superiority (and popularity) in the future.

Remember that an organizer's purpose should be to keep track of everything you need to do and to allow you to focus on performing work instead of worrying about it.

7. Delegation is prime in determining your effectiveness. The quality of your work also depends on your ability to properly delegate. Delegate properly and you'll multiply your productivity. Remember, when you delegate, you are assigning another person a task to do and the authority to do it. You don't hand over control or accountability. These stay with you.

8. Make follow-up and follow-through part of the process of work. You can do this by including it as part of the weekly review process as you meet regularly with each of your direct reports. Remember, too, that these weekly meetings are the time for your staff to follow up with you on input you're expected to supply. If follow up and follow through work both ways, these meetings will become predictable, useful times together that will help everyone do their work better and more efficiently.

CHAPTER 6

Do It *Right*, Now!

*You can't escape the responsibility of tomorrow
by evading it today.*
—ABRAHAM LINCOLN

Chapter 6 Preview

In this chapter, you will learn:

- To check what the customers' expectations are and fulfill those needs. It isn't enough to do what you think is important.
- To improve the process of your group's work, begin with the process of your personal work.
- To make dramatic improvement, you must abandon your old ways of processing your work and start using new methods to introduce more effective ways of working.

So far we have been addressing how you process your personal work. In some cases you may improve a work process you already have in place. In other cases you may completely change some aspect of how you do your work. The process of work is the central theme of all quality and reengineering efforts. Whereas quality improvement concentrates on the continuous, incremental improvement of existing processes, reengineering focuses on discovering and implementing completely different and new processes. Both efforts have realized tremendous success in improving productivity, especially in the manufacturing industry. No doubt your company either has one of these efforts underway or is considering it. A personal efficiency program (PEP) is the perfect complement to your quality and reengineering drive. PEP and quality and reengineering complement each other. You must use the principles of quality improvement and reengineering to dramatically improve your own personal productivity.

THE ORIGIN OF PEP

In the early 1980s, I was living in Sweden and had a small sales and marketing consulting business. To attract new clients, I devised a compensation plan unique to Sweden: I wouldn't accept a fee unless the client got a measurable result. It had an attractive ring to it, and I found it pretty easy to get companies interested and to be willing to at least see me and listen to what I had to say. If a potential client thought I had something to offer, the first hurdle to overcome was figuring out what constituted a measurable result. Since I specialized in sales and marketing, I often was able to work out a measurable target, usually increased sales and customers.

The next challenge I faced was creating a marketing and sales campaign that would deliver that measurable result. This was easier than I imagined: All I had to do was ask the people who did the work what would they do to increase the desired result. Most of the time they knew what to do.

I would develop a plan based on their input and give it to them.

Now this is the interesting part: Almost invariably I would return to find that the plans hadn't been executed. The staff members didn't have time. They had too many other things to do. Someone got sick or went on holiday. This posed a problem for me. I had to get them to do the plan or I wasn't going to get paid. The workers were caught up in day-to-day inefficiencies, wasting time looking for things, being disorganized in hundreds of ways, and my main duty became not my "wisdom" with sales and marketing but getting the principals well organized so they could do the things they had been thinking about doing all along.

I succeeded to build up a client base. One of my clients was a branch of Svenska Handelsbanken, one of the most profitable banks in Sweden. It hired me to increase the amount of money in savings accounts. The measurable target was to increase the amount of money in savings accounts. Along with the management team and staff, I worked out a marketing plan to accomplish this target. Then the hard part—getting it done.

At Svenska Handelsbanken, several things were keeping the plan from being implemented. For example, as a matter of policy, the bank personnel periodically rotated jobs and workstations. As a result, every few months people found themselves at a new workstation without knowing where things were. It took a few weeks to attain some semblance of order. Meanwhile, time was wasted.

Instead of processing each transaction immediately, some cashiers would create huge backlogs by putting aside until later the tasks they thought would take longer. Cashiers who processed each item of work immediately, as it happened, didn't develop backlogs.

Since there were no baskets on the desks, when mail came in, it sat on top of the desk with all the other papers. Sometimes individual items from the day's mail were buried beneath other papers and overlooked entirely.

The branch manager was a competent executive, but she spent most of her time dealing with customers. This gave her little time to devote to the organization of the individual workers.

I started a standard filing system at each desk and purged the place of clutter. That way, if someone had to use a workstation he or she was unfamiliar with, at least he or she knew where to find things. I asked the senior cashier to describe how she processed her work. This became the model for processing transactions in the bank branch, and the other cashiers began following her model. We set up a central mail center with baskets for each worker. Soon the staff were initiating their own solutions to common problems affecting their productivity. Eventually the bank hired me to package for them what I had done in this one branch and train fifty internal trainers to deliver the Personal Efficiency Program to their 500-branch network.

I learned from this experience and from the many other clients in Sweden and a dozen other countries in Europe and North America that the vast majority of people are proficient and technically skilled to do their work but they don't understand the principles of work organization or the application of these principles to their jobs.

Work process improvement is understood by most to be improvement of the computer system or the manufacturing process. Most individuals are only vaguely aware of a personal work process, and they seldom, if ever, address this personal work process.

It drove home a familiar point: If you can't manage yourself, how can you expect to manage others? This is true too, of our attempts to dramatically improve the productivity of our group through total quality or reengineering. If you can improve how you process your own work, if you can change how you behave, you have a much greater chance of successfully changing the work process of the group.

The greatest success I had in improving group productivity came from focusing on the basics of the personal work process. Most people don't give much thought or assign much importance to the work process. But once they begin to work on _how_ they do their work, they often continue without my encouragement because they become much more productive. William James, the famous nineteenth century philosopher, said: "what a person puts their mind to happens."

PEP—A PRACTICAL TOOL FOR QUALITY IMPROVEMENT

At one division in General Motors, a client said:

The quality gurus build awareness here, but PEP makes time management and organizational efficiency workable because it's done on the job, at the desk, and this is practical.

The act of improving _how_ you process your work will give you visible and immediate results. The results encourage you to extend your methods to other processes and give you the fortitude to continually improve these work processes until you achieve success. It also gives you the _time_ to focus on improving the broader work processes.

4S

A Japanese approach to the subject of quality only recently coming to the attention of the West is called 4S. 4S is the label for

SEI-LI	Organization
SEI-TON	Orderliness
SEI-KEZ	Neatness
SEI-SOU	Cleanliness

4S actually comes from the Chinese, but has been successfully copied and implemented by the Japanese. As described by Ingrid

Abramovitch in an article entitled "Beyond *Kaizen*", in *Success Magazine* (January/February, 1994, p. 85), 4S goes beyond *kaizen*, the better known quality concept of continuous improvement. *Kaizen* focuses on manufacturing processes, whereas 4S "takes a grass-roots approach, helping each individual to attain the highest level of personal effectiveness."

Wellex, a US-based manufacturer of computer circuit boards, has employed 4S in its operation and realized a productivity increase of more than 26 percent in less than two years. The president of Wellex, Danny Lee, saw 4S in action when visiting Japan. In August 1991 he visited Miyoshi Electronic, a company much like Wellex. "The first thing I saw," says Lee, "was that their facility was clean and neat, compared to ours. They have a very small factory, since space is so expensive in Japan, and over one hundred kinds of assembly running simultaneously. Yet everything was so organized. Their employees seemed to be concentrating. And all the workstations were so neat." The attention to detail and the plant's spotlessness were no accident, according to Ms. Abramovitch. This was 4S.

The employees of Miyoshi structured their work around the steps of 4S: "Organize your materials. Perform the job in an orderly fashion. Clean up afterward."

As one Wellex employee describes it, "(4S) is much more basic for employees than quality. TQM [total quality management] comes from the top down; 4S from the bottom up. To implement one, you need the other."

There is a process (how you do what you do) that needs to be addressed and improved if you are to do the right thing, now. You do this by concentrating on the components of 4S and bringing order to your environment and the way you work.

IDENTIFYING YOUR CUSTOMERS AND THEIR NEEDS

I run into an interesting phenomenon in delivering the PEP program. In conducting before and after surveys to establish measurements for success and to get feedback on our own work, I ask PEP participants how they have personally benefitted from the program. Typically, 85 to 90 percent of our clients make excellent personal progress and the results are more meaningful because they are so personal.

Another question we ask in the survey concerns their perception of how their coworkers have done with PEP. The answers to this question are much more mixed. People tell us, "Well, her desk isn't that clean anymore." "I still don't hear back from Sam fast enough." We found that PEP had made the participants more capable of accomplishing the things that were important to them, but they weren't necessarily meeting the needs of the people around them. Since that time we have asked the participants to find out what their coworkers expect and need and to make the satisfaction of those needs one of their objectives. It is a great success.

The lesson to be taken from this is that it's not only important to produce what you think is important but also to produce what others perceive as important to them. You have to find out from your colleagues, coworkers, all of your "customers," both internal and external, what they consider to be important. Not only does PEP enable you to know what your customers need, being well organized enables you to respond better to those customers' needs.

> *It takes less time to do something right than it takes*
> *to explain why you did it wrong.*
> —ANONYMOUS

BENCHMARKING

Benchmarking, the comparing of what you do with the best of a class, is a critical tool for improving quality. The comparison tells you how well you're doing and, usually, how to improve. The PEP process first defines excellent personal work systems and organizations and then provides that benchmark for individuals to compare how they process their own work.

Like the senior cashier in the Swedish bank, a select few in your group may develop efficient and effective ways to get their work done. Use these people as your own models. They are known as master performers. If there is a gap between your high and average performers, identify how your high performers execute their work and what behaviors allow them to produce better than their average coworkers.

FOCUS ON PREVENTION

PEP moves you from a reactive mode to a proactive mode. Putting good planning processes in place enables you to look into the future and prevent problems. It makes you aware of those red flags and indicators that could become fires in the future. Not only are you aware of them, but with a *Do It Now* frame of mind, you act on these things while they're manageable and you can prevent serious problems from occurring.

PROJECT-BY-PROJECT IMPROVEMENT

Joseph Juran, an American quality consultant who introduced management systems that plan, control, and improve quality, emphasizes the need to improve quality by using project-by-project improvement plans. Dr. Juran stresses that management's role is to provide planning and guidance to improve quality. Translating quality concepts into action at every level is management's job.

Management's role is to help improve the skills and knowledge of their staff to plan work and accomplish actions that will improve quality and increase productivity.

CONTINUOUS CHANGE

People have a very difficult time dealing with change. And yet, continuous improvement is all about continuous change. Top executives can dictate but most effective managers prefer to involve their people.

Continuous change is hard to deal with if personal goals and desired end results are not clearly stated and regularly reviewed. Project management, time management, work space-organization, follow-up and follow-through are all components of continuous improvement.

From a PEP perspective, quality improvement has three main ingredients:

1. Identify what needs to be improved.

2. Plan out the actions to improve it.

3. Push the plans through.

PEP AND REENGINEERING

The most dramatic benefits from PEP have come from people who have decided not simply to improve what they do, but to revamp their work completely and start fresh. You probably see many ways you can reengineer your work but may not implement them unless your desire to change and your persistence are strong. In their book *Reengineering the Corporation* (HarperCollins Publishers, Inc., 1993), Michael Hammer and James Champy suggest you must question why certain things are in place and question your assumptions and beliefs if you expect to make dramatic changes. To illustrate what some of your assumptions about personal work management might be, I'll use Hammer and Champy's belief/response/solution format from *Reengineering the Corporation*.

Belief: One has to operate on the basis of priorities.

Response: This is only partially true. I recommend you get rid of the little nagging things periodically and efficiently, since they make it very difficult to focus and concentrate on the real priority items.

Solution: Set up an efficient process to first eliminate the things you get that shouldn't even cross your desk. Secondly, process your day-to-day activities in an efficient and timely manner so you can concentrate the bulk of your time on the important priorities.

Belief: Planning is a waste of time because new things constantly come up and interfere with the plan anyway.

Response: Without planning, you spin your wheels, have no direction, and do things out of sequence. The result is that things take much longer to do—so long that the time is consumed by other issues that catch up with you. If you are inefficient at the planning process it will take longer than it has to and discourage you from planning.

Solution: Identify key objectives you're responsible for and, with whatever tools you're most comfortable with, (preferably a computer or other electronic solution), create specific project plans for each of them. This way, you can monitor and oversee the things you need to get done in an organized way. Make planning an efficient process.

Belief: If a cluttered desk equals a cluttered mind, what does a clean desk equal? The assumption is that to be creative one has to be disorganized and messy.

Response: Creativity does not depend on clutter. To get things done, you have to be well organized and have processes and systems in place to allow you to do that. Create creative time.

Solution: Organize your working environment so you have the time for creativity. Identify "creative" time and put yourself in an environment that is conducive for you to work creatively.

Belief: I'm too busy trying to get my job done. I can't afford to take the time to write everything down—it gets in the way of my work.

Response: All work has inherent in it a preproduction phase. To the degree that you get a clear picture of what it is that you need to do, you get it done faster and better. Writing things down forces you to articulate and get a clearer picture.

Solution: Schedule a time weekly as your organizing and planning time. Introduce that as part of your work systems and habits and test ways to make it as efficient a process as it could possibly be.

Belief: He went to college. He should know how to handle his papers efficiently and work effectively in an office.

Response: Because people go to school does not guarantee they know how to work or they have good work habits. People on average waste up to 50 percent of their time due to poor work habits.

Solution: Place emphasis on the improvement of the personal work process. Put staff through a PEP type program.

By examining your assumptions, you can begin to identify ways to do what you do differently or not at all.

REENGINEERING AND TECHNOLOGY

As mentioned previously, two of the major complaints I hear repeatedly are first, that too much time is consumed in meetings, and second, that people could finish their work if only *other* people would do their share of the project on time. Few old solutions to these two problems have ever worked. That makes both of these areas prime candidates for the reengineering process.

Imagine reducing meeting time by 75 percent.

Imagine people dealing with their share of the work concurrently so you didn't have to wait to be able to address your own work.

Technology has come to the rescue on these two very difficult and deep-rooted problems in the white-collar environment. Groupware software and shared databases now exist so people can communicate with each other on issues that previously would have required in-person meetings. Everyone can contribute information from their personal perspective through a PC network, cutting down dramatically on the need for face-to-face meetings and the time they waste.

I'm not saying that meetings will be eliminated completely. This is neither necessary nor desirable. Face-to-face human contact remains essential. But the ability to cut down on this time-consuming contact while substituting other, more efficient (and yet satisfying) ways of sharing this information, can eliminate a major source of wasted time.

Another convenience you enjoy through networking and groupware is that you can share information with others at any time and not have to wait for a scheduled meeting or to get the person on the line.

Much of the need for follow-up and the delays you face in completing the things you need to get done are wrapped up in how your work group may be organized. In their book, *Reengineering the Corporation* (HarperCollins Publishers, Inc., 1993), Michael Hammer and James Champy state that the way to eliminate bureaucracy and flatten organizations is to reengineer processes so they are no longer fragmented.

Too often work is done sequentially. As an individual, you might finish one part of a project and have to wait for someone to finish a related part before you can begin working on the next step. Even if you use the parallel design process to overcome this particular problem, this method has its own problems. As described by Hammer and Champy, the "parallel design process" involves many people working on different parts of a bigger scheme at the same time.

"Usually," say Hammer and Champy, "the sub-systems will not fit together because even though all the groups were working from the same basic design, changes, often improvement, occurred along the way but were not communicated to the other groups." (p. 45) Then it's back to square one in designing the product. This dilemma is eliminated by having technology in place that facilitates and makes it possible for people to work concurrently on issues with knowledge about each other. At the same time, via technology, people are able to communicate any changes introduced so the consequences of those changes are immediately known to all involved.

In my experience in delivering PEP to thousands of people, most people move the route of continuous improvement of their existing processes. They are more comfortable introducing incremental changes and improving existing systems. But the dramatic gains available to you through PEP most often come when people take a radical and completely different point of view of how to address their work. These radical approaches almost always depend on the use of technology. The greatest gains from PEP come to those who embrace the planning process and change how they do what they do and who put organization and planning at the forefront of their work. To really succeed with PEP, you have to put organization and planning into all of your routines in a complete way.

FOLLOW-UP FOR CHAPTER 6

1. PEP has the potential to be a critical success factor for you and for your company. PEP addresses how you process your work. It isn't enough to be proficient and technically skilled to do your work; you have to understand the principles of work organization and the application of these principles to your job.

2. Quality improvement concentrates on continuous incremental improvement of *existing* processes. Reengineering focuses on discovering and implementing completely different and *new* processes. You will find both methods useful in improving your personal productivity and the productivity of larger groups with which you're associated.

3. PEP not only has the ability to help you with things that are important to you as an individual but also the things that are important to the people around you. One of the objectives of PEP is to enable you to satisfy those expectations and needs, as well as your own.

4. Select a model you can use as a benchmark in improving your efficiency and effectiveness.

5. Examine your assumptions for mis-assumptions. You can then make the decision of whether reengineering or quality improvement is the next step in improving any given work process.

The *Do It Now* Manager

*If you wait for people to come to you, you'll only
get small problems. You must go and find them.
The big problems are where people do not realize
they have one in the first place.*
—W. EDWARDS DEMING

Chapter 7 Preview

In this chapter, you will learn how to:

- Successfully get others organized.
- Best use of your new-found time.
- Employ one of the most effective means of delegating work.
- Practice effective management with the principle of "walking around."

I once delivered the Personal Efficiency Program (PEP) at a manufacturing plant in England. The participants included managers, administrators, and shop supervisors. I had several PEP coaches with me to facilitate the program; in fact, my participation was limited to introducing the concept and getting a few participants started. One supervisor was particularly enthusiastic about the prospect of getting better organized. He wanted to know all about PEP and how he might use it. I told him, "If you think PEP is good for you, wait until you see what it can do for the people who work with you."

I suggested that the most effective use of his new-found discretionary time would be to move around the shop floor to visit with his people every day and to find out firsthand from them what they needed to get themselves better organized and produce what they needed to produce.

When I returned to the manufacturing plant a few months later, I was approached by the same supervisor. He excitedly described his experience with PEP. He asked if I had known about the strike that occurred in the plant the month before. I told him I had heard about it but didn't know the details. He asked, "Did you know that the whole factory went on strike except for my section?" He said that when senior managers looked into why his was the only section not going on strike, they found that the employees in his section had no complaints. They said that all of the things that they had felt were wrong had been dealt with and handled by the supervisor during the previous months.

What this *Do It Now* manager did is described in this chapter.

MANAGEMENT BY WALK ABOUT

One of the most important tools a manager has to get things done effectively and efficiently is a technique called Management By Walk About (MBWA), or as some call it, visible management, or management by wandering around.

Through the process of MBWA, getting around to my people and seeing what they had to deal with and what problems they faced, I created the PEP program.

Years ago I worked as a manager in a business where the employees were under tremendous pressure to supply services, produce products, and get them out the door. I was responsible for some two hundred people. A typical day consisted of meeting with the senior management team to discuss internal issues and meeting with customers, then doing lots of paperwork, primarily to satisfy the reporting demands of the higher executive levels. My job was a study in crisis management. I seldom, if ever, was able to leave the office.

But then two things helped me change that. First, I got myself organized. I had help in establishing routines with my secretary and I began to deal more effectively with the paperwork I was responsible for. Second, I used the time resulting from my reorganization to get out of the office and practice management by walk about. I spent nearly half the day every day getting out to visit with every single person I was responsible for. I would stop at their desk or work area, sit down, and chat with them to find out how things were going. I soon realized that most of the people were working extremely hard, but they were not being very efficient or effective in their work. The general scene was one of disorder.

When I first started MBWA, people were suspicious. They wondered why I was there and what I was looking for. But this suspicion quickly went away when they found that I would come back regularly and that I showed a genuine interest in what they were doing. Soon they began to open up and address long-term productivity issues. I listened intently to what they had to say and tried to respond to their expressed needs.

If I didn't respond to a need, I felt very uncomfortable facing the person again. MBWA forced me to be effective in dealing with the issues that were brought up, especially those issues that I wholeheartedly agreed should be dealt with.

I discovered that most of the people I managed had no idea how to work effectively. It wasn't that they didn't work hard: in fact, they obviously worked much harder than they really needed to. That's when I discovered that if I could help them do something to improve how they did their work, I would get the most results from my efforts as a manager.

This was MBWA, with a twist. Yes, I listened; yes, I responded, but I also coached them how best to organize themselves and get on top of what they needed to do. I coached them on how to organize and improve their work processes. I helped them improve their organizing skills and apply them to their work environment. This was not just lip service: I visibly coached and facilitated the process. I would not only listen, I would look. After noticing a disorganized condition, I would try to discover the underlying causes. What I often discovered was that people could no longer see their actual working conditions.

For example, I might ask a man to clean out his desk. Once he had finished the task, I would look at the desk. And more often than not, I would find that things were overlooked or not even seen in the first place by him.

I have come to believe in black holes, or at least, in the black hole phenomena in organizations in which you send something out and it seems to get lost, never to be seen again. Well, those black holes are usually in desk drawers and files. Things simply get shoved away without being dealt with.

Why aren't many important items dealt with? The reasons are many: bad working habits, procrastination, not knowing exactly what to do, poor planning, poor organization, crisis management, and many more. Interestingly enough, rarely do I find that bad intentions or lack of effort are the cause of production difficulties. Often people do not have the authority to handle the problems they face. Or they find things difficult to address, even though another person might find the same things very easy to deal with. Or they feel that every direction they turn, they run into a wall, so they give up trying.

Often I find that arbitrary rules, poor policies, and inefficient work processes create these negative feelings in people. Eliminating these rules and creating new standards almost always improve the morale and productivity of people. What seems like insurmountable and intractable problems to them are, in most cases, within the supervisor's ability to handle. For example, if someone on staff needed a computer to process her work better, I could authorize the purchase immediately, have procurement get it fast, and allow the person to get on with her work with the resources that she needed.

Through MBWA I discovered an extremely effective way to coach people in their jobs. I did this by going through their pending files with them. We would go through each piece of work, one by one, and have them process it then and there. In the pending files, I found procrastination, misunderstanding, and arbitrary rules that prevented people from doing the things they needed to get done. I would have never found these problems simply by asking because, as is often the case, if people had known what the problem was, they would have resolved it. I had to see the process and how they worked, to notice that they didn't have the necessary tools, or that they experienced many disruptions, or what was making the work difficult to do.

Within a very short period of time in this management position, I experienced something I had never before experienced—visible results, not only to me, but to everybody. The office became much neater. Things were labeled. Common files became comprehensible and useable. People began to take pride in their surroundings. They began to work together to solve the problems that made their work harder to do. The more I concentrated on the basics of work, the more visible the results became.

The more time I spent out of my office with the people who did the work—discussing, looking, testing, resolving, eliminating blocks to production, coordinating—the more real production results we achieved and the easier it was to achieve them. This was a complete revelation to me then.

Having since seen how many other companies work, I know that MBWA is not used by executives and managers to the degree it could be. Countless times as a consultant I have been told by people that their boss has never been to their office. Most managers merely pay lip service to the MBWA concept.

I challenge you to use the time you gain through PEP to be out and about with your people and become a *Do It Now* manager. That is PEP's greatest payback. Let us look at why.

AN EXAMPLE OF MBWA

One of the most effective executives I know runs a bank in Luxembourg. He consistently out performs his peers chalking up 20 to 25% return on equity, year after year, in good and bad times.

He has a flat table desk with no drawers located in an open office environment. He processes his work immediately. He delegates liberally. You seldom find him at his desk because he spends most of his time around the seven floors of the business. He hates meetings so has few of them. Those that he has are held before or after banking hours and are therefore brief and to the point.

He hates clutter and makes this known when he sees it. He has a rather large turnover of staff (theirs is a foreign bank in Luxembourg and they regularly rotate staff from the home office for training and experience), so his message to new and old staff: be orderly; be quick; don't accumulate; get it done, now! His concentration is on the basics and he demonstrates this visibly. That is MBWA.

WHY MBWA WORKS

Many success factors come as a result of MBWA. Being out and about, you see and hear things you otherwise wouldn't see and hear. Being out and about prompts you to ask questions and improves your communication and listening skills. Most difficult problems don't go away at the first attempt to deal with them; but, by being out and about with your people, you get their input. You find yourself following up and addressing the problem and testing solutions.

Staff productivity problems are too often affected by things out of their control. To resolve these problems, people who work in other divisions may have to cooperate, even though they have their own priorities. As the manager, you are the only person who can bring these groups together and work out solutions. If you have been out and about, you know the real issues and can help push through solutions.

Another reason why MBWA works is simply because people receive much-needed attention. Remember reading about the study done in the late 1930s by a company called Western Electric? They conducted an experiment on improving productivity in the workplace. They found that if they turned the lights up on the factory floor, productivity went up. Then they tested to see what would happen when they turned the lights down on the factory floor. Interestingly, productivity went up again. One conclusion drawn from this study was this: when attention is placed on the needs of people, production increases, even if the things getting attention aren't the right things.

If you are out and about, attending to the issues and needs of the people producing the products, productivity will improve. If in the process of MBWA, you concentrate on the right things, your rewards are that much better.

FACE-TO-FACE COMMUNICATION

Our pride often makes it tough to talk about our failings, especially when communicating with our bosses. What might be obvious to others, may not be so visible to us. These blind spots create a division or gulf between management and the people doing the work. The best way to bridge the gap is to communicate one on one, face-to-face. When you are talking about the same issues on the same level in the same space, you communicate more effectively. MBWA creates these golden opportunities to communicate. You encourage open communication when you ask people how they work, what they are doing, and what things will make their lives and jobs easier. *Do It Now* management means being out there with people, asking questions and making observations that enable you to comprehend, to listen, to learn.

When I'm out and about in my work, I often ask PEP participants to give me a brief statement of the strategy of their operation. The senior executive of one PEP group was shocked to find that none of the participants in the group, except for himself, could state what the strategy of the operation was. When he and I discussed the matter later, he told me that he thought everyone knew about it. The company had published an annual report about it for all the world to read and in two staff meetings he had covered it in detail.

I didn't find any of this very surprising. In all the years I've been working with companies, only once or twice have I found that employees had any real clue of the strategies being worked on by the company. Too often the companies didn't have a strategy at all. And in companies with a strategy, the communication of it was poor at best.

If you have a message to get across, if you have a plan to get done, if you are trying to execute a strategy, or if you want to explain your vision of the future, there is no more effective method I know than meeting face-to-face with your people.

A *Do It Now* manager communicates the vision and strategy of a company continuously through his or her actions as well as words. If the company's strategy is to get the competitive edge through dramatic improvement in the quality of customer service, the *Do It Now* manager demonstrates this by actions on the front line with the people who are dealing with the customers and often with the customers themselves. All aspects of communication are greatly enhanced through MBWA.

FOLLOW-UP METHOD

Chapter 5 discussed the importance of follow-up and follow-through. With MBWA, you schedule follow-up and follow-through into your work process. Being out and about with your people is a natural way to follow up and follow through on the things that you want to get done.

DELEGATION

When I talk with executives about their failures to delegate, the most common reason I hear is how busy their people are and how overwhelmed they would be if they were given any more to do. This perception is often formed by seeing the person's desk piled with papers or by hearing how late he or she stays at the end of the day. MBWA gives you a much more accurate sense of how much work your people do. Moreover, you can see how the work might be spread out differently. My experience suggests that when a *Do It Now* manager is out and about, he or she ends up delegating much more and much more effectively.

WHAT DOES A *DO IT NOW* MANAGER DO?

A *Do It Now* manager provides the resources, encouragement, coaching, and training people need to produce what they need to produce, in as effective and efficient a way as possible. A *Do It Now* manager does this by visibly getting around on the front lines of the business.

CONCENTRATE ON THE PROCESS OF WORK

To be effective as a *Do It Now* manager, you should first and foremost focus on the process of the work. In my experience, sufficient pressure is placed on staff to produce, but rarely is sufficient pressure put on how the work is produced. As a *Do It Now* manager, if you help people to concentrate and focus on the process of work, you will ensure that their job continues to improve and things get easier for them. This focus gets them to resolve core issues and at the same time improves the quality of the product being produced.

What do you look for? Are the people well organized? Do they have files that are easy to use, for themselves as well as the people around them? Do they have the tools that they need to produce and are these tools operational? Are they employing good working routines? Do they procrastinate? Do they plan? Do they see where they fit into the grand scheme of things?

The most effective way to produce change is through small and incremental steps. There is no need for a *Do It Now* manager to overwhelm his personnel with too many things at once. Asking them to deal with and handle one small piece of the puzzle at a time and following up that it has been done is all that is usually needed. Again, it is very difficult facing your people again, after you may have promised to resolve some issue and failed to do so. The solution? Deal with it. Handle the issue. And until it is handled continue to keep on visiting the person and letting them know what it is that you are trying to do and what you are running into.

BUILDING TEAMS

In the course of employing visible management, it's not uncommon to discover that individual issues are impacted by members of the team. Also, it's common to find divisions of people within the organization. After all, this is how most organizations are structured. Visible management is an opportunity for you to get clarity on what individuals make up the team and the process of work. You are then better able to reorganize both the process and the team. Visible management is an effective tool in the reengineering process. You can greatly enhance team activity in the organization by eliminating the barriers between the team members. Without visible management, it is very difficult to isolate those arbitrary rules and barriers that can prevent the team from functioning properly.

DON'T BE TIED TO THE DESK

One senior manager, responsible for a division of nine hundred people in a large manufacturing firm, strongly felt that MBWA was one of the most important things he needed to do. But he said that he had no time to do it. He was constantly dragged into other problems, meetings, and crises. He felt tied to his desk.

The solution that he and I worked out was relatively simple. He would spend the whole morning out and about at different sites where his people were located and wouldn't even come to the corporate office until 1:00 in the afternoon. Interestingly enough, with a little bit of organization, screening of information that came to him, improved delegation, and elimination of waste of time, he was able to get out of the office earlier each day, and still put in the extra 4 or 5 hours getting around to his people.

Being "tied to the desk" is a common complaint from executives. Simply scheduling MBWA before sitting down at the desk works for some. A more permanent solution is to get rid of the desk completely. One manager did so and operated his business with a clipboard. Not having a desk forced him to get out and about with his people nearly full time. When he had an important meeting, he would hold it in the office conference room.

In his book *Thriving on Chaos* (Alfred A. Knopf, Inc., 1987), Tom Peters tells a story of another manager who got rid of his desk and used a small work area in two departments, a round table with three chairs, and a filing cabinet in an open area by the entrance door. This allowed him to work better with his secretarial support and to handle his mail more efficiently. I like this idea. If you don't have a desk, you don't have a place to store extra papers and materials that you will never use anyway.

START WITH YOURSELF

It is human nature to see the cause of one's difficulties "over there." But many improvements can be made within your own area at little or no cost. This experience is common when employing quality improvement processes in companies. If you go after the red herring—a new $9 million computer system when you don't have the money or it will take two years to install it—you will miss the hundreds of improvements you could make in the interim.

ELECTRONIC TOOLS TO ENHANCE MBWA

As a manager, you likely have a few layers of management between you and the front lines. Bypassing those can create problems. One solution is to bring them with you, electronically. One way to do MBWA is by using electronic tools. If you can't get around often enough to your people, electronic tools can help.

E-mail is one such tool. Inviting employees at all levels to communicate both problems and suggestions directly opens the lines of communication. Your physical presence in their area periodically makes E-mail that much more effective.

For smaller businesses, networking software allows you to communicate directly through PCs without having to invest lots of money. Lotus Notes, one such software application, is easy to customize for your business. The customized databases can be accessed by anyone authorized in any geographical location with a telephone. Anyone in the organization can participate and contribute to important issues and questions put forward by yourself or others. Most telephone companies offer their own E-mail services and as long as you have a PC and a modem it is possible to communicate.

CLOSING THOUGHTS ON MBWA

If you are a senior manager, you might think that you have a nearly impossible schedule as it is. Where are you to get additional time in the day to walk about? Sam Walton, the brilliant mind behind the building of Wal-Mart, the largest retail store chain in the world, spent about 80 percent of his time out and about in his stores. He reportedly traveled four days a week visiting the stores and spent one day in the office. With revenues topping $70 billion, you can be certain Sam could have kept himself occupied in an office. He chose to do otherwise. By being out and about, he solved many management problems directly and greatly reduced paperwork and other time-consuming activities such as devising policy, setting strategy, dealing with the budget, contacting customers. Sam found that these roles are more effectively carried out with the input of those who have to do the work.

The question then, is not how much time you have, rather, it is how you use it. Is it important to you to practice visible management? Is it important to you to know what is going on in the front lines?

The most effective use of management time is getting out and about with people every single day. If you concentrate on the process of work and make it easier for your people to produce, you will do much toward accomplishing the vision, strategy, and goals of the operation.

FOLLOW-UP FOR CHAPTER 7

1. Schedule a block of time in your day to get out and about to your areas of responsibility. The most effective time may be first thing in the morning. If so, don't even bother to come into the office until after you have made the rounds *visibly*.

2. Concentrate on the process of work and how it may be improved.

3. Communicate the vision. Know the strategy of your operation and communicate that strategy in actions and words. Help your people envision where your operation is going.

4. Deliver on what you promise. If you say you are going to do something for an employee, *do it*. If you find it's difficult or impossible, get back to the person and let them know where you stand. Do everything in your power to keep your word.

5. Focus on helping your employees improve teamwork when you are out and about.

Maintain It Now

The time to repair the roof is when the sun is shining.
—JOHN F. KENNEDY

Chapter 8 Preview

In this chapter, you will learn:

- A task is done when you have put everything back in better condition than when you picked it up.
- The less you keep, the less you have to maintain.
- The purpose of good maintenance is to make it easy to produce next time.
- To add tasks to each weekly plan that will create improvements in your work situation.

An associate once told me of a young man whose parents gave him a new car when he turned eighteen, to celebrate both his high school graduation and his first "real" job. Although the young man made a point of having his car washed once a week, he never changed the oil in the car. Naturally, when this simple, routine maintenance step was skipped repeatedly, the car's engine parts began to grate and grind against one another. Eventually, the entire engine locked up. The result was a burned out engine and a useless car, all because ordinary maintenance hadn't been done.

Beyond the loss in monetary terms, what struck me was the foolishness involved and the fact that it needn't have happened at all. Here was a boy who had neglected the most basic and practical of car maintenance procedures, ignoring routines that should have guaranteed a smoothly operating car for years to come.

As I mulled over this story, I thought, perhaps the parents never taught their son the importance of changing the car's oil. My hunch, though, is that they simply *assumed* he knew how important it was and that he was changing the oil regularly. It's such a basic, integral part of car maintenance, it may not have crossed their minds that he might not be changing the oil.

People have a very low awareness of maintenance in their administrative work. Executives, when cornered to explain their lack of action on the subject, "expect" their people to know these things because "they're professionals." If they think about it at all, they assume someone else is working on it, so they do not demand it be done.

We know the consequence for that boy. The consequence for not getting and keeping yourself and your people organized is far more severe than a locked up engine.

MAINTENANCE AND THE WORK CYCLE

I learned a lesson about maintenance from an old-timer who worked for IBM. He would travel to customer sites and repair their mainframe computers. He would often have younger technicians with him on these jobs. He was the butt of jokes because he had "peculiar" clothes and work habits. He used to wear overalls with dozens of pockets in them. In his pockets were all the different tools he needed or might need. If he saw something to be repaired, even if it hadn't been part of the original repair order, he'd repair it. If he saw a drop of oil on the ground he took out his cloth and cleaned it up, then and there. As he used a tool he cleaned it and put it back in the appropriate pocket. If a tool broke, he had a requisition form in his pocket that he filled out right then to replace the tool. His colleagues would attack the job not bothering to clean up as they went and inevitably when the end of the day came the old-timer was always done and ready to go before the others. This was his way of working. He maintained an organized state.

Simply stated, maintenance is part of the work cycle. Think of it this way: Each piece of work, each task, has a beginning, middle, and end. Part of the task beginning must include organizing (planning, preparing for, setting up) for the task. In the middle is the act of doing the task. Finally, along with task completion, the ending must include maintenance points, including "put things back where they belong," and "improve the condition of everything you touch" (including files, tools, and so forth).

Maintenance routines should be thought of in the same way. The easiest way to do this is to incorporate basic maintenance routines into your work cycles, in exactly the same planned way you change the oil in your car. In the same automatic way you slide in behind the wheel, insert the car key, and start the engine, you know that the car's oil must be changed on a routine basis if your car is to be in top shape. Why should you expect work to be any different?

For example, how might you handle the job of answering a letter from a regular client? You should start with the client's file, so you have the client's past history of association with your company at hand. You can then refer quickly, easily, and accurately to any pertinent facts. You can verify the spelling of names based on materials sent to you from the original sources. You should be able to cite dates, based on copies of invoices or order forms. You would have copies of all earlier letters to refer to. You'll likely discover "resources" you didn't know exist.

The point is, by going to the client's file, you don't risk embarrassing yourself (and your company) by being uninformed. What you know influences what goes into the letter, and the quality and content of the letter is likely to be greatly improved.

Assuming you're using a paperwork process, when you complete a letter and get ready to put it into your out box, what do you do with the client's file? You take one or two minutes to put it into order. Sort letters into chronological order, with the most current letter on top. Eliminate duplicate letters. If there are loose business cards in the file, staple them to the folder itself so they don't fall out of the file and become lost. Or file them in the Rolodex. Two minutes, tops! And when you put the file back, it will be in better shape and more current than it was when you picked it up. That's maintenance.

This maintenance routine applies to your computer files as well. If the composed letter is in the client's directory, quickly glance through the rest of the directory, purge any unneeded documents and organize what's left. A colleague of mine found 1,800 messages in someone's groupware database. No one can use that much information or keep up with it. His client simply didn't organize (or more likely, didn't delete) as he went along. Time is not the issue. The issue is making organization part of the work process.

MAKE IT EASY

The purpose of maintenance is to make it easy for people to produce.
If the copy machine runs out of paper while you're making copies, fill
the machine to a functional level. Don't put a dozen sheets in the tray
so you can finish your job and leave the next person to run out of
paper. Don't leave your files in such a hopeless state that no one,
yourself included, can hope to make sense of them. Instead, turn
everything you touch into a tool for increased efficiency and
productivity.

Maintenance means organizing yourself in a way that makes forward
movement easy. If you empty your stapler, refill it. If you reach in
your drawer and you're out of staples, go to supply now and get a
box of staples. Fill your stapler and get on with your work. Don't
leave small details hanging unsettled, so they trip you up at a later
time. Few things are as frustrating when trying to take a telephone
message as reaching for a pen and not finding one or going through
half a dozen before you find one that actually works. If a pen is out of
ink, throw it away; pens are meant to be disposable.

SHOULD YOU BE MAINTAINING IT IN THE FIRST PLACE?

For maintenance to continue, it has to consume as little of your time
and effort as possible. Otherwise, being human, you're going to find
yourself putting it off "until it's more convenient," or you're "not quite
so tired," or "when you have the time" or whatever excuse you may
find not to do it. Therefore, you want maintenance to be both efficient
and painless.

If you've been thorough in purging your files, you'll have little
(or at the least much less) to maintain. If you discover that you are
spending time maintaining something you seldom if ever use, you
have to question its worth to you. Start questioning why you're
maintaining it. If it's something you can honestly do without, do
without!

MAINTENANCE AND *DO IT NOW*

If you have taken to heart the concept of *Do It Now* you will have ample opportunity to reinforce it with maintenance. Why? Because maintenance isn't always the most "important" or most "urgent" thing to do. There will always be reasons to postpone a maintenance action. But if the words *Do It Now* pop into your head when you first recognize some maintenance action, you will act. If you see some tool needs repair, you will *Do It Now*. If a supply runs out you will fill it immediately. *Do It Now* becomes the habit and it extends itself to maintenance.

MAKE MAINTENANCE A HABIT

Just as you automatically brush and floss your teeth in the morning it's best and easiest to establish nonthinking, efficient maintenance routines in your work. As covered in Chapter 3 batching and scheduling the processing of your paperwork and E-mail daily keeps your day-to-day work flow under control. A weekly organizing time can be incorporated into your weekly planning process to maintain your organized state. Bring your filing up to date. Back up your hard drive. Check on your supplies.

Just as you've scheduled a time each day to empty your in tray, you should schedule a time for the big jobs that are so tempting to put off, such as purging your files of any unnecessary clutter they may have accumulated. I have often found people do this sort of complete cleaning of the office at the end of the year, usually between Christmas and New Year's when it seems everything slows down in the office. They use the time to get rid of the old year's papers, set up the next year's files, purge what they haven't used lately, get rid of the stacks of magazines they saved to read, and generally clean up. While this is better than not doing it at all, it is in my experience, not enough. Purging and cleaning on a quarterly basis seem to work best. Schedule it in your calendar, say half a day. Close the door and get to work reorganizing, purging, going through all of your books, reference files, archives, and such.

Figure 8.1 shows a schedule for maintaining your system.

MAINTENANCE AND TRAVEL

I'm on the road most of the time. I travel overseas monthly and in the United States once or twice a month. By choice, our office has no secretary. We organize ourselves and cover for each other. The idea of how to do this came from a small company in Sweden and has served us well since.

We have had to use electronic tools as well as services from the telephone company to keep in touch. We make it a practice of calling the office every day and processing what has come in, over the telephone. We have had to organize ourselves to do this. Whoever is in the office keeps all incoming correspondence at hand under each person's name. As one of us calls in all of the correspondence is quickly gone through. Normally we respond to this correspondence immediately by telephone from where we are. You can believe this is a fast process because telephone costs are high and we don't care to waste money. If a fax needs to be sent, the person in the office sends

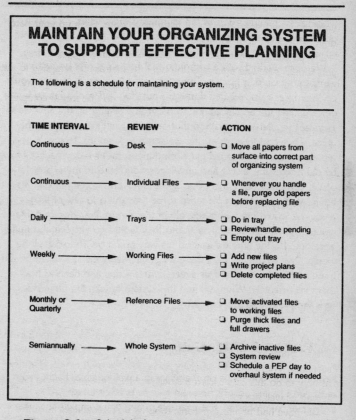

Figure 8.1. Schedule for maintaining your organizing systems.

it. If there is junk mail we throw it away. Some items can only be dealt with when we return, but they turn out to be much less than would otherwise be there. This system has worked very well in all companies it has been introduced to.

One executive never schedules a meeting for exactly when he returns. He always allows himself a few open hours upon return to wrap up everything from his trip (summary of activities, receipts, any offers he may have to prepare as a result of the trip) and get caught up with all that has accumulated while he was away.

We once worked with a company that had sales representatives working out of their homes. They organized their week so they would do their sales calls Monday through Thursday and spend Friday in the office getting the administration in order and setting up the new week. The reps regularly complained that one day was not enough in the office. They had to work on the weekend to keep up. However one rep always managed to get his work done in the five-day period. How he did it was simple. He had envelopes addressed to the regional office, corporate office, his boss, accounting, and home office in his briefcase. As something came up to be forwarded to one of those places he would put it immediately in the appropriate envelope. He would process his receipts daily and they would go into the accounting envelope. By the time he was on his way home on Thursday all he would have to do was mail the envelopes. Meanwhile he called in and handled his phone messages several times a day and dealt with all of them immediately. When we put this system in with the other sales reps the problem disappeared.

PREVENTIVE MAINTENANCE

Not only must you focus on maintaining a well-organized state, you must consider the actions you can take to prevent future organizational problems. For example, when you complete this year's tax return, set up a file for the new year. As tax-related information arrives during the year, file it immediately. If you plan ahead, and start the tax preparation process early, collecting the necessary information during the year, you won't panic around March and April when it's due.

You can also identify peak periods during the year and organize yourself to deal effectively with those periods. Early preparation can lessen the burden when those peak periods arrive.

MAINTENANCE AND CONTINUOUS IMPROVEMENT

Even after all of the times I used the word "maintenance" in this chapter, it is not precisely what you should be concentrating on. Yes, an end product is to prevent you from backsliding into old, nonproductive habits. It isn't enough however, to PEP yourself up and then only concentrate on keeping things that way. You also have to work to make things better. You should work conscientiously and deliberately to improve how you do your work. In today's fast-paced competitive environment it isn't enough to do better and stay that way. You must continue to excel. Even if you've made considerable progress, your real goal should be continuous improvement in everything you do.

I've mentioned that people seldom include tasks on their To Do lists that are geared toward improving how they complete their work. It isn't that people aren't thinking about these things. In fact, with quality and reengineering drives underway in most companies, many people are thinking about exactly these things but not in relation to their day-to-day work. Instead, they think of continuous improvement in terms of maintaining the plant's No Defects product record for a year.

Every week I make it a point to ask myself the question, "What will I do in the next week to improve my work situation?" There have to be several tasks on my weekly plan that will make my work life easier, make me more effective, increase my knowledge, or in some way change the way it is to a better way.

I might add a task to read two chapters from a software application I'm interested in expanding my use of. I have seen people choose tasks from their personal improvement goals and schedule them into their work calendars. I encourage people to add those spontaneous ideas that come up and act on them. "Learn how to use that new printer" might be one. We all have a thousand and one things we would like to do or get to make things better. Well, do them!

Include these objectives in your weekly plan. Schedule them. You will discover that you tend to figure out how to get them done in the least amount of time. Because the task is there, you act on it. Better yet, gradually and continuously your office is not only keeping its new image and efficiency, it is improving it.

You are making change part of your everyday life. And you are the one directing the change.

PERIODIC CATCH UP

Some people don't feel the need to maintain their organization minute-by-minute. They may not care to. They have successfully kept pace with their workload by periodically catching up on their organization. If in the middle of a project or peak period they will keep up as best they can, at the end of it they can spend the time they need to get themselves back in order. A few important things to consider if you decide to work this way. Do not allow more than a couple of weeks to go by before you get reorganized. You should be very thorough about your cleanup. Keep very good reminder systems in place so important things don't fall between the cracks.

MINIMUM MAINTENANCE

Once you're organized, the minimum maintenance you should do (which is better than nothing): Clean off your desk each day before you go home.

WHAT TO DO WHEN IT ALL GOES TO POT?

So okay, you have purged your desk and office and it looks like the cockpit of an F-16 aircraft. You are organized like never before. You finally got into a routine that keeps your day-to-day flow of paper, messages, information, E-mail, and so forth under control. You plan your work each Friday. You bought a notebook computer and have begun to learn an organizing software, and you feel pretty good about yourself. You are cruising along and bang; you run into a brick wall! You are called to Tokyo to replace a colleague for six weeks. Or a big customer puts your account up for review and you need to prepare a presentation to salvage it and you are off for two weeks straight, 16 hours a day dealing with that. Or you go on vacation and come back to backlogs and a mess all over again. Something like this will happen to you. And let me tell you, you'd better be clever with how you respond.

In my experience, people do not fall back into their *new* ways. No, chances are they slide back into old habits. And face it, you managed to cope with your old ways, right? It has probably been a real struggle to get organized. To have to do the personal efficiency program (PEP) all over again! It was a good try, but you're just not the organized type. Believe me I have heard all of these. Don't despair or give up. There is an easy and painless way to deal with this. Have a *Do It Now* day. Put a sign on your door saying you are off for the day, pile all of your papers on your desk and go through the process again. It is much easier and takes far less time than the first time you did it. Maybe a few hours and your paperwork will be under control again.

To make this *Do It Now* day easier, try to keep up with your daily flow of information anyway. If you are having to spend your days getting the presentation prepared, take an hour of that time and blast through what has come in the day before. Delegate liberally, then and there. Be decisive (even ruthless) about what you are not going to do. Use (and maintain) your tickler system to get papers off the desk and in their proper place. Take advantage of the circumstances to see how efficient you can be and when you are back to normal, keep that same pace!

It may never get this bad for you. But the work flow usually shifts and you may find yourself beginning to drown. One client, a director for one of the largest industrial firms in the world, described it this way:

When work builds up and momentarily gets on top of me, I know what to do to deal with it because I have learned the necessary procedures.

You now have learned the procedures too.

Maintenance means recognizing the inherent cycle within every piece of work you do, from preparing yourself to do the work to putting everything back where it belongs after the work is completed, and guaranteeing that everything is in as good or better condition than when you first picked it up. Maintenance means organizing yourself while you work.

The most important thing to maintain is change for the better.

FOLLOW-UP FOR CHAPTER 8

1. Recognize maintenance as the most basic and practical of work routines, and you'll be guaranteed a smoothly operating system for years to come. Make it a point to practice basic, practical maintenance routines that will guarantee the hard work you've put in to "get PEPped" will pay off for years to come.

2. Make your maintenance routines automatic, exactly in the same planned way you change the oil in your car. It's worth your time and effort to establish nonthinking, daily routines to maintain yourself and to maintain an organized state. Failure to maintain the system will result in an inability to work at all.

3. Have systems in place that will prevent you from falling back into old ways. Have routines that trigger continuous personal improvement and help you maintain those system as a matter of course. Schedule it into your week.

4. Remember to think of work to be done in terms of work cycles. Each piece of work has a beginning, middle, and end. The task beginning includes preparing and setting up for the task. In the middle is the act of doing the task. Along with task completion, the ending includes maintenance points, including putting things back where they belong, and improving the condition of everything you touch, including files, tools, and so forth.

5. Realize that the advent of the computer means paper files aren't the only things that require maintenance. We now have computer files, and E-mail, as well. Maintaining your hard drive means having backup systems and using them regularly, so your electronically stored data isn't at the mercy of a sudden power failure.

6. Set a weekly organizing time to keep your long-term flow of work under control. Spend time each week planning for the coming week and maintaining your organized state. Get your filing up to date. Back up your hard drive. Check on your supplies. Use a quarterly, annual, or other schedule for maintenance to keep your maintenance on track and up to date.

7. If you discover you're spending time maintaining something you seldom use, seriously question its worth to you. If the reason you're maintaining something doesn't make sense to you, let that be a red flag to you. Ask why you're maintaining it. If it's something you can honestly do without, do without!

8. Organize yourself while you work. Make maintenance a part of the planning process and you'll be including it from step one to step done. Plan for success. Establish good habits. Make maintenance a nonthinking habit, and you'll find it's a easy step on your road to success.

9. Don't get comfortable! Your real goal should be continuous improvement in everything you do. PEP is a tool, or a framework, to allow you to accomplish it.

EPILOGUE

Just One New Habit

> *What characterizes a well-adjusted person is not*
> *chiefly the particular habits he holds, but rather the*
> *deftness with which he modifies them or responds to*
> *changing circumstances. He is set to change, in*
> *contrast to the more rigid, dogmatic, self-defense*
> *individual who is set to sit tight.*
> —WENDEL JOHNSON

You may find very little profound thought in these pages, but there is
a great deal of experience.

In essence, we have discussed the way you have conditioned
yourself to approach your work: your habits. Most people will tell you
(and I dare say too many of us believe) that it is very difficult to
change habits. It isn't easy. But it can get better. It is possible to adopt
new ways of doing things, to develop new habits in your life. You
may have experienced walking into a new restaurant out of curiosity
or by accident, and having found you like it, you may make a point to
return again and again.

It all begins by adopting one new habit, that of taking action. *Do It
Now* when the idea crosses your mind to test out a new method for

doing your work. Try driving to work on a different route when the idea strikes you.

The "bad" habit isn't necessarily "being messy." The bad habit includes constantly neglecting the habit's correction—never doing a thing about it. Break that cycle and act on it now rather than postponing. You will find you'll have it licked in no time. It's up to you to act on your ideas as they occur. You will discover you can indeed be the master of your habits.

INDEX

Should you wish to order a free copy of any of the forms found throughout this book or purchase the PEP Planner software (both individual and groupware) please write or call:

The Institute for Business Technology International Inc.
P.O. Box 1057
Boca Raton, Florida 33429, USA
Telephone (1) 407-3670467
Fax   (1) 407-3670469

If you would like more information about the Personal Efficiency Program or if you would like to speak with a PEP representative, contact one of the following Institute for Business Technology offices:

The Institute for Business Technology, Australia and New Zealand
P.O. Box 331
North Sydney NSW 2059, Australia
Telephone (61) 2-9553269
Fax   (61) 2-9555480

The Institute for Business Technology, Benelux
P.O. Box 688
1180 AR Amstelveen
Halfrond 429 Westelijk
1183 JD Amstelveen, Netherlands
Telephone (31) 20-6473752
Fax   (31) 20-6477633

The Institute for Business Technology, Canada
19 Donegani, Suite 604
Pointe Claire
Quebec H9R 2V6 Canada
Telephone (1) 514-6319207
Fax   (1) 514-6947892

The Institute for Business Technology, Denmark
Lungso Alle 3
DK 2970
Horsholm 400 Denmark
Telephone (45) 45-762511
Fax   (45) 45-762520

The Institute for Business Technology, Germany
Flurstrasse 47
D-63073 Offenbach am main, Germany
Telephone (49) 69-891090
Fax   (49) 69-891009

The Institute for Business Technology, Norway
Gamle Brevik VEI-1
N-1555 Son, Norway
Telephone (47) 64-959225
Fax   (47) 64-959162

The Institute for Business Technology, Sweden
Formskararegatan 9
S-412 61 Gothenburg, Sweden
Telephone (46) 31-814190
Fax   (46) 31-814360

The Institute for Business Technology, Switzerland/France
Case Postale 339
1224 Chene-Bougeries, Geneva, Switzerland
Telephone (41) 223-497963
Fax   (41) 223-492423

The Institute for Business Technology, United Kingdom
P.O. Box 95
Redhill
Surrey RH1 IYG, England
Telephone (44) 73-7768415
Fax   (44) 73-7768560

The Institute for Business Technology, United States
513 Capital Court NE, Suite 100
Washington, DC 20002, USA
Telephone (1) 202-5440097
Fax   (1) 202-5446898